How to Teach Poetry Writi Workshops for Ages 8–13

Now in a fully revised and extended second edition, *How to Teach Poetry Writing: Workshops for Ages 8–13* is a practical and activity-based resource of writing workshops to help you teach poetry in the primary classroom. Designed to help build writing, speaking and listening skills, this book contains a wide selection of workshops exemplifying a variety of poetry styles and showing how their unique features can be used to teach key literacy skills. This book includes:

- redrafting and revising activities;
- poetry writing frames;
- traditional and contemporary poems from a range of cultures;
- poems written by children about their favourite subjects;
- word games and notes on performing poetry;
- cross-curricular links;
- new workshops on performance poetry, wordplay, rhyming and un-rhyming poetry and narrative poetry;
- an A–Z guide to poetry.

Featuring a wealth of poems and a new bibliography to help you find the perfect poem for a lesson, this book will be of interest to all teachers looking to develop the necessary skills in their pupils to become confident writers of poetry.

Michaela Morgan is a practising poet, children's author, writer and former teacher. She runs workshops and courses in the UK and internationally.

5b

Also available in the Writers' Workshop Series:

How to Teach Writing Across the Curriculum: Ages 6–8
Sue Palmer
(ISBN: 978-0-415-57990-2)

How to Teach Writing Across the Curriculum: Ages 8–14
Sue Palmer
(ISBN: 978-0-415-57991-9)

Speaking Frames: How to Teach Talk for Writing: Ages 8–10
Sue Palmer
(ISBN: 978-0-415-57982-7)

Speaking Frames: How to Teach Talk for Writing: Ages 10–14
Sue Palmer
(ISBN: 978-0-415-57987-2)

How to Teach Poetry Writing: Workshops for Ages 5–9
Michaela Morgan
(ISBN: 978-0-415-59013-6)

How to Teach Poetry Writing: Workshops for Ages 8–13

Developing creative literacy

Second edition

Michaela Morgan

Routledge
Taylor & Francis Group

LONDON AND NEW YORK

First published 2001 as *How to Teach Poetry Writing at Key Stage 2*
by David Fulton Publishers

This edition published 2011
by Routledge
2 Park Square, Milton Park, Abingdon, Oxon, OX14 4RN

Simultaneously published in the USA and Canada
by Routledge
270 Madison Avenue, New York, NY 10016

Routledge is an imprint of the Taylor & Francis Group, an informa business

© 2011 Michaela Morgan

Typeset in Helvetica and Sassoon Primary by FiSH Books, Enfield
Printed and bound in Great Britain by MPG Books Group, UK

British Library Cataloguing in Publication Data
A catalogue record for this book is available from the British Library

Library of Congress Cataloging-in-Publication Data
Morgan, Michaela.
How to teach poetry writing : workshops for ages 8–13 : developing creative literacy / by Michaela
Morgan. — 2nd ed.
  p. cm. — (Writer's workshop series)
1. Poetry—Study and teaching (Elementary) 2. Creative writing—Study and teaching. I. Title.
PN1101.M643 2011
372.62'3044—dc22

2010029695

ISBN13: 978-0-415-59014-3 (pbk)
ISBN13: 978-0-203-83298-1 (ebk)

Contents

Acknowledgements		*vi*
Introduction: Writers' Workshop		1
Almost Everything You Need to Know about Poetry Workshops: A–Z		5
Workshop 1:	Licensed to Thrill – performing poetry	18
Workshop 2:	Monday's Child – rhyming couplets	22
Workshop 3:	The Day the Zoo Escaped – redrafting	27
Workshop 4:	Every Word Counts – careful word choice	31
Workshop 5:	Fin Flapper – kennings	35
Workshop 6:	Waves – shape/concrete poetry	38
Workshop 7:	Further On – idioms and word play	42
Workshop 8:	Space Rap – performance poetry	47
Workshop 9:	The Robin – rhyming and un-rhyming poetry	50
Workshop 10:	The Poem Hunt – the senses	52
Workshop 11:	I Am a Baggy T-Shirt – metaphor	56
Workshop 12:	The Sound Collector – onomatopoeia	59
Workshop 13:	Nocturnophobia – personification	63
Workshop 14:	Three – levels of meaning	66
Workshop 15:	December – poems reflecting different cultures and voices	71
Workshop 16:	Hubble Bubble – comparison of different treatment of classic and contemporary themes	77
Workshop 17:	The Charge of the Light Brigade – classic narrative poetry	82
Workshop 18:	The Dead Quire – challenging narrative poetry	90
Appendix		95
Bibliography		*97*

Acknowledgements

We are grateful to the following copyright holders for permission to reproduce their material:

Roger McGough, for 'The Sound Collector', from *Pillow Talk* (Viking, 1990), reprinted by permission of Penguin Group Ltd.
Roger McGough for 'On and On' from *Lucky* © 1993 Roger McGough, printed by permission of United Agents (www.unitedagents.co.uk) on behalf of Roger McGough.
Carol Ann Duffy, for 'Three', from *Hello New* (Orchard Books, 2000), © Carol Ann Duffy by kind permission of the author c/o Roger, Coleridge & White Ltd, 20 Powis Mews, London, W11 1JN.
Valerie Bloom, for 'December', from *Let Me Touch the Sky* (Macmillan Children's Books, 2000), © Valerie Bloom.
Chatto & Windus for 'Mama Dot' by Fred D'Aguiar, from *Mama Dot* (Chatto & Windus, 1985). Used by permission of the Random House Group Limited.
June Crebbin, for 'The Robin', from *The Crocodile Is Coming* © 2005 June Crebbin, reproduced by permission of Walker Books Ltd, London SE11 5HJ.

Every effort has been made to trace copyright holders, but in some instances this has not been possible. The publishers would like to apologise for any errors or omissions, and would appreciate being advised of any corrections that should be made to future editions of this book.

The author would like to acknowledge the help and inspiration of the poems, books and workshops of the following:

John Cotton
Roger McGough
Brian Patten
Kit Wright
Sandy Brownjohn

Introduction: Writers' Workshop

Writers' Workshop

A scribble of writers scrabbling for new ways,
Crossing out and changing, making blots of mistakes.
Herd of oxymoron in the background brightly snoring.
A litter of alliteration on the look out, lying low.
A chorus could come in, chanting, chanting.
A repeated refrain here and there, here and there.
Metaphors are matadors, they add their flourishes,
Similes wait like actors in the wings.
A scribble of writers now searching for an ending.
A question? Or a shock! Or a gentle fade . . .
Reach for the tools to hammer out those sentences.
A workshop of writing waiting to be made.

Michaela Morgan

Making a start

Reading, hearing and enjoying poetry

Reading aloud, listening and *enjoying* are the essential first steps to writing poetry. Regularly read poetry aloud to your class and to yourself – just for the poem, not for any follow-up work or to make any point. *Poem for the Day* or a good anthology (see Bibliography, p. 97) will provide a wealth of varied poetry.

Reading a poem aloud just before a break, or to start or finish the day, will not eat into your time very much and will help to hone the ear and increase the breadth of acquaintance with poetry.

The book or individual poems should be displayed and readily available for those who want to re-read the day's poem.

Encourage children to find favourite poems and to read them aloud to you, the class or each other. Enjoy the *music* of language as well as its meaning.

Honing the ear and all the senses

From time to time, take a few moments to listen or stand and stare. Ask the class to say or note down what you and they can see, hear, touch, taste or smell, and try to find a descriptive word or simile to capture these observations.

Complete silence in the classroom is necessary for the listening time. Silence is 'when you hear things'.

Note the smallest of noises – also what you *imagine* you can hear (e.g. *I hear a ticking, tick tick tick – the clock? or the teacher's pen? or the brain clicking as it thinks?*).

Teachers and/or teaching assistants should join in this activity – to be seen quietly concentrating, scribbling, crossing out etc. provides a good role model – and you will enjoy the activity!

Making a word hoard and writing together

When you have started on a poem, gather words and ideas in a whole-class or group session. Jot down all suggestions on a flipchart or interactive whiteboard.

Link words that go together because of their rhyme, alliteration etc.

Compose whole-class poems together before considering sending children off to write individually.

Sometimes, take existing poems and omit words or phrases. Discuss which would be good words or phrases to insert.

Reading aloud

Reading aloud is an excellent chance to hear how/if a poem is working. This is a chance to consider making changes.

During a writing workshop, pause to read rough drafts aloud, applaud them and consider revisions.

Redrafting and revising

The first drafting of a poem is a beginning; changes and improvements can be made. Do whole-class or group redrafting sessions on whole-class poems. Demonstrate the process of crossing out and changing, discussing reasons for the changes. Things to consider are: deleting unnecessary words (poetry is economical); changing words for onomatopoeic, alliterative or other more powerful words; tightening rhythm or rhyme; altering word order to put emphasis on important words or to avoid having to stretch for a rhyme; punctuating.

Being more specific and detailed can help a poem. Instead of 'we sat under a tree', consider what *sort* of tree: 'we sat under the willow' or 'we sat under the oak'.

Poetry is less painful than a story to redraft. Writing poetry encourages experimentation with word choice, word order etc.

Making a collection

Making a class anthology is a wonderfully useful and enjoyable activity. Choose a theme or poetic form or just let children find any poem they like. They copy their poem out (or key it in). Copying a poem sharpens their understanding of it. You often notice much more about a piece when you have to write it exactly as the poet has written it. Why is that punctuation there? Why is that line broken there?

Each child can read his or her chosen poem aloud and try to explain what they like about it. Some children could learn their poem by heart. The heart is a good place to keep a poem.

Cross-curricular links

Links can often be made between poetry and the topics covered in the rest of the curriculum. A poem on the subject under study can be used to introduce the theme. The whole class can write a poem on their current topic using the knowledge they have gained. Acrostics are easy to use to summarise a subject.

For an example of a whole-class rap that has summarised a study of the solar system, see Workshop 8, 'Space Rap', on page 47.

Put on a poetry performance

Poems can be performed individually or in groups. Children can be encouraged to learn a poem by heart and practise their performance of it. Performances can be accompanied by music or props or images. They can be recorded or filmed.

Performances can be put on the school website or on the Perform a Poem website (http://performapoem.lgfl.org.uk). See Workshop 1, 'Licensed to Thrill', on page 18.

Invite a poet

Consider inviting a poet into school; this can really make a difference to the profile and enjoyment of poetry in your school. Try for a poet whose work you have enjoyed – approach him or her through the publisher, or through a specialist contact agency (details below).

The children can then hear a poem in the poet's voice and talk about it. Maybe the poet will run a workshop or sign copies of his or her books.

Prepare for the visit by reading some of the poet's work and follow it up by displays and readings.

Give children the opportunity to buy copies of the books, to make the poems their own. If this is difficult, financially, you should ensure that the poems are bought and are available to all in the library or classroom.

Some useful contacts to help you find a poet to visit your school:

- Contact an Author: www.contactanauthor.co.uk
- Class Act: www.classactagency.co.uk
- NAWE (directory of writers): www.artscape.org.uk
- The Poetry Society: www.poetrysociety.org.uk

Your local library service, arts organisation or bookshop may also be able to offer useful help.

Tools of the trade

Make sure you have:

- a rhyming dictionary (Penguin publish a good one);
- a thesaurus (again, Penguin publish an excellent thesaurus – Roget's, or you may prefer to opt for a thesaurus specifically targeted at children);
- a large and good selection of books of poetry, including rhyming and un-rhyming, and classic and contemporary. (See my recommended websites and bibliography for some suggested titles.)

And finally... Why write poetry?

The skills involved in writing poetry are transferable to all types of writing. All writing benefits from careful word choice, detail, keen observation, use of the senses, thoughtfulness and awareness.

Word games and verse hone specific writing skills.

Poetry requires revisions and redraftings. All writers, particularly young ones, can become downhearted having to revise longer pieces of writing, but the brevity and focus of poetry makes writing appealing, achievable and fun. Poetry is playful – it encourages experimentation.

And, most importantly – poetry is creative and enjoyable, so have fun!

Almost Everything You Need to Know about Poetry Workshops: A–Z

A

Acrostic

A very popular poetic form in schools. The title of the poem (e.g. 'Holiday') is written vertically and provides the initial for each line:

H
O
L
I
D
A
Y

For cross-curricular links choose your current topic as the subject for an acrostic, e.g. Evacuation to link with study of World War 2 or Diwali, Christmas etc. to link with study of festivals.

If you are going to write an acrostic, do some examples as a whole-class activity first and demonstrate the gathering of ideas before writing each line. Consider what makes a holiday, for example resting, lying in bed late, sunny days, ice cream and lollies, taking it easy etc. Then try to include some of the things you want to say in the acrostic:

Happiness is our hope
On our holidays.
Lying in bed all day,
Idling, lazing, dreaming
Dozing . . .
All the time in the world . . .
Yes!

Advertisement poem

Advertising agencies think very carefully about their advertisements, some of which have poetic qualities (rhyme, rhythm, alliteration and onomatopoeia are particularly popular devices). Look at advertisements, then try writing ones that tempt the reader to eat oranges, go swimming, read a book etc.

Make cross-curricular links by producing advertisements linked to your current topic, e.g. healthy eating.

Alliteration

Words beginning with the same sound (not necessarily the same letter – as in *free phone* or *one wonderful wombat*). Used frequently and to enormous effect by the Anglo-Saxons, alliteration remains widely used today in poetry and song. It is an effective way of binding words together and making music with them.

Alphabet poem

Take a subject and write an A to Z of it. For example, if you were to take 'Cat' as your subject, you could write a poem composed of adjectives:

> **Athletic, balletic, cosy cat.**
> **Daring, energetic, furry cat.**

or verbs:

> **I am Cat.**
> **I attack, I bite, I curl, I dance...**

Cross-curricular links can be made by writing an A to Z of your current topic.

Ambiguity

Deliberate ambiguity is an excellent device in poetry. Unintentional ambiguity ('The secretary went down to the kitchen and brought up her dinner') can have quite a different effect.

Assonance

Subtler than rhyming, it is a repetition of sounds to make a half-rhyme, e.g. *crying time.*

B

Ballad

The ballads of Robin Hood or 'Sir Patrick Spens' are examples of traditional ballads. They tell a story in a regular, usually four-lined ('quatrain') form with a regular rhyme scheme (typically *ab ba*). A modern example of a ballad is 'Timothy Winters' by Charles Causley.

Brainstorming

When brainstorming for words, accept all offerings and note them. Then select from those submitted, giving reasons for your choice, e.g. *'This has a sharp sound'* or *'I like the alliteration here'.*

C

Calligram

The formation of the characters, or the font, represents something of the word's meaning (e.g. **SHOUT!** or *whisper*). See Workshops 6, 'Waves' and 8, 'Space Rap'.

Cinquain

Cinquains have five un-rhyming lines and a total of 22 syllables, in the sequence 2, 4, 6, 8, 2. This form was invented in 1911 by Adelaide Crapsey. Writing a cinquain gives experience of very careful word selection in a poem that does not usually rhyme.

Concrete poem

Another term for a shape poem. (See Workshop 6, 'Waves'.)

Confidence

An essential! Try not to be tempted into decrying even 'silly' or 'rude' suggestions during brainstorming times. Out of mischief, creativity can creep. Acknowledge successful poems – or lines or even words. Be tactful with revision suggestions.

Joining in with saying poems will increase speaking confidence. Writing poems as a whole class will increase writing confidence. The writing frames also provide helpful support.

As a teacher or teaching assistant, make sure you build up your own confidence too. Try out the workshops and have a go at writing a poem yourself.

Conversational

Many, or rather most, poems are in a particular poet's voice, as if the poet is having a conversation with you. Read Michael Rosen's work for examples of work that captures the rhythms and vocabulary of everyday language, situations and conversation.

Couplet

Two consecutive rhyming lines. (See Workshops 2, 'Monday's Child', and 3, 'The Day the Zoo Escaped'.)

D

Dialogue

Don't forget that dialogue can be included in poems: in fact, entire poems have been made of dialogue. Try 'Ghosts' by Kit Wright in *Rabbiting On*, published by Young Lions.

Diary poem

Try a diary of a goldfish – plenty of scope for repetition, refrain and changing word order to make slight differences! A Days of the Week poem provides a supportive structure and can be linked to a variety of topics (food, countries etc). A Days of the Week poem can take a very simple form ('On Monday I danced in France. On Tuesday I took a plane to Spain'. . . etc.) or can be much more thoughtful (see Workshop 2, 'Monday's Child' on p. 22, which includes the poem 'Mama Dot' by Fred D'Aguiar).

E

Elegy

A lament, usually for the death of someone.

Empathy

To stand in the shoes of someone else and imagine and write how it would feel. Poetry taps into the imagination, creativity and empathy of human beings in a way that transcends anything you can target or assess.

Epic

A long story or poem of heroic endeavour. Classic examples are Homer's 'Odyssey' and 'The Iliad'.

Epitaph

An attempt to sum up a life in a few words. An epitaph usually starts with *Here lies...* You will find a wealth of them in *The Faber Book of Epigrams and Epitaphs*, where you will note that they often use word play to humorous or critical effect. The Earl of Rochester's epitaph on King Charles II is fairly typical:

> **Here lies our Sovereign Lord, the King,**
> **Whose word no man relies on;**
> **Who never said a foolish thing,**
> **Nor ever did a wise one.**

Probably best attempted as the summation of the life of a typical figure (e.g. a figure representing a profession, such as a teacher), rather than of an individual, they can be complimentary or funny or cruel, as in one I prepared earlier:

> **Here lies a footballer,**
> **whistle blown on his last game.**
> **He kicked the bucket, not the ball,**
> **and was never seen again.**

F

Figurative language

Use of simile, metaphor and similar devices.

Form

Providing a form for writers to follow can provide a release and a starting point for writing – but feel free to adapt the form. It should be a supporting framework, not a straitjacket. Don't let unfamiliarity with poetic forms intimidate you – if you want examples of every poetic form, use *The Works: Every Kind of Poem You will ever Need for the Literacy Hour*, chosen by Paul Cookson and published by Macmillan.

Free verse

Verse freed from the need to rhyme or adhere to a fixed metrical pattern. Free verse has words carefully chosen for reasons other than rhyme and rhythm.

G

[Have a] GO!

Poetry is all around us and is one thing everyone can have a go at. Even those who 'don't like writing' can love poetry. Anyone who can enjoy word play in jokes, or who enjoys rhythm and sound in music can write a poem – and enjoy it!

H

Haiku

A traditional Japanese form of poem, which encourages a careful and economical choice of words, based on an awareness of syllables. Every word, every syllable counts in a haiku. Every line-break has to be carefully considered. Haiku is a very brief form but it requires great control. It is an exercise in making restrained choices with language It can help jolt a writer away from usual rhythms, pounding rhymes and well-used vocabulary. (See Workshop 4, 'Haiku'.)

A haiku always has 17 syllables. It consists of three lines only. Line one has five syllables, line two has seven, and the third and last line has five. A brief moment in time is captured in a clear visual image. *The Penguin Book of Japanese Verse* provides many examples. (See also **Tanka** on page 14.)

Link a haiku workshop with a cinquain workshop to help children grasp syllable counting.

I

Idiom

Everyday figures of speech (e.g. 'keep an eye on your sister'). They are not to be taken literally! For examples, see the poem 'Figuratively Speaking' in the appendix and Workshop 7, 'Further On', on p. 42.

Imagery

Use of language to capture or create a mental picture of something.

Internal rhyme

Rhyme within a line, as in *'You peel and you grapple with orange or apple'*. Internal rhyme can also be within a word, as in *hubbub*.

J

Jokes

Jokes and word play alert us to language. Jokes can rely on puns, homophones, spoonerisms etc. for their effect. They, and tongue-twisters too, are little steps towards poetry. (See word game suggestions on http://www.everybodywrites.org.uk/writing-games/primary/)

K

Kenning

Found in Norse and Old English poetry, a kenning is similar to a riddle, as the thing described is not usually named but described in compound expressions, usually of two words (e.g. *fast forgetter, ankle-biter*). (See also Workshop 5, 'Fin Flapper'.)

Cross-curricular links can be made by linking the writing of kennings to your topic, e.g. a kenning about rivers or the wind to link with Geography. For history, write kennings about historical artefacts (e.g. a Viking sword, an Egyptian mummy).

L

Limerick

A light-hearted exercise that can be done as a group or class activity as well as independently. The finest examples are probably those of Edward Lear. The famed *Anon* also wrote a large number of limericks!

Line-breaks

It's worth taking a well-known poem and writing it out as continuous prose. Then, with the class, have a go at breaking it into lines. This is the best way of alerting an apprentice writer to the choices and possibilities line-breaks provide.

List poem

Think of a subject and list its qualities:

Christmas is ...
dark nights
bright lights
rising hopes
[etc.]

Encourage children to put unexpected, witty or well-described things in their lists. If they keep to a carefully controlled number of words in each line, they have a **Thin poem** too! (see entry below).

Cross-curricular links can be made by writing list poems on your current topic, e.g. for Festivals, a Christmas list poem (see example started above) or a Diwali list poem.

Literacy Hour

Poetry fits wonderfully into the Literacy Hour. A whole poem rather than an extract from a book can be read as a starting point. Writing can be a whole-class, group or individual activity, and the plenary time is a perfect opportunity to read aloud, perform, listen attentively, discuss, applaud and consider revisions and improvements.

M

Metaphor

A figure of speech in which one thing is said to be another. An example of this is in the poem 'Writers' Workshop' on page 1: *Metaphors are matadors, they add their flourishes ...* (See also Workshop 11, 'I Am a Baggy T-Shirt'.)

Monologue

A poem can be written as a monologue – one person or one animal or one object talking. Cross-curricular links can be made by writing a monologue by a historical figure (e.g. a Viking speaks or a Roman speaks or Florence Nightingale etc.).

N

Narrative poem

A narrative poem tells a story. Ballads are narrative poems. (See Workshop 17, 'The Charge of the Light Brigade' and Workshop 18, 'The Dead Quire'.)

Near-rhyme

Near or half-rhyme can give wider choice and subtler effect than full rhyme, e.g. *summer/dimmer.*

Ngu Utu

A Japanese form of poetry that alternates lines of five and seven syllables in a poem of any length, ending with two rhyming lines of seven syllables. Link with writing of Haiku,

Tanka and even Cinquain, to help children master economy, word choice and syllable counting.

Nonsense poem

Nonsense poems are wonderfully liberating. I suggest 'Jabberwocky' by Lewis Carroll, who invented *portmanteau* words in this *tour de force*. Also read poems by Spike Milligan.

O

Observation poem

As the name suggests, these are based on observation. Take the time to stand and stare – to really look, hear, taste, smell and feel. You could start *'Through the window I see . . .'* (See Workshop 10, 'The Poem Hunt', on p. 52.)

Onomatopoeia

An interesting word in itself! Made up of two Greek words for 'name' and 'make'. Words like *hiss* that make the sound they are describing are onomatopoeic. (See Workshop 12, 'The Sound Collector'.)

Oral poetry

Children will be acquainted with a range of oral poetry that they can be reminded of – jingles, playing songs, nursery rhymes. All poetry was once oral – epics and ballads were composed as poetry to make them more memorable before writing became widespread. The oral tradition continues strongly today. Continue the tradition by encouraging children to read poetry aloud and perform their poetry. (See Workshop 1, 'Licensed to Thrill'.)

Oxymoron

An apparent contradiction as in *bitter-sweet* or *gloomily gambolling*. There is an example (*brightly snoring*) in the poem 'Writers' Workshop' on page 1.

P

Performance

> Truly fine poetry must be read aloud. A good poem does not allow itself to be read in a low voice or silently. If we can read it silently it is not a valid poem: a poem demands pronunciation. Poetry remembers that it was an oral art before it was a written art. It remembers that it was first song.
>
> Borges

Actually, I think some very good poems can be read silently, but on the whole I agree with Borges. Poetry benefits from being read aloud. Read aloud! Perform! (see http://performapoem.lgfl.org.uk).

Personification

Language that gives objects human emotions or attributes, e.g. *'The trees dripped with sadness...'* (See Workshop 13, 'Nocturnophobia'.)

Poem

A poem is many things, some of them contradictory:

It can be direct – a quick connection to the heart, the memories, the senses.
It can be indirect, subtly hinting.
It can be moving, mysterious, sad, serious, comic, crazy, funny.
It can be downright nonsense.
It can explode. It can whisper. You can join in and clap and sing, or whisper it softly in your own mind.

Coleridge defined a poem as 'the best words in the best order'. In a poem, language is used with awareness. Pope's famous adage, 'What oft was said but ne'er so well expressed', sums it up. It's not just *what* you say but how you *say* it. Poetry is generally (but not necessarily) economical with language. The main thing is that it is a source of delight!

Q

Quatrain

A four-line stanza.

Question-and-answer poem

Ask everyone to write a question (a wide-ranging one such as *What is the sun?*) Then try to answer the questions – not factually.

R

Rap

A form of oral poetry that has a very strong rhythm and regular rhyme. (See Workshop 8, 'Space Rap'.)

Recipe poem

A poem that imitates the form of a recipe. (See Appendix, 'Recipe for a Story'.)

Refrain

A repeated line, or group of lines, in a poem can help to bind it together. (See Workshop 16, 'Hubble Bubble'.)

Renga

A series of haiku each linked to the next by two seven-syllable lines. Sometimes a poet would write a haiku and send it to another poet who would link it and add his or her own haiku – making a sort of letter poem. (See also Workshop 4, 'Haiku'.)

Rhyme

The reading of poetry of all sorts will demonstrate that it doesn't have to rhyme. That said, rhyme does have an enormous attraction. *But* if you are in danger of being forced into writing something pointless or silly, something that breaks the mood or lets the poem down, abandon the rhyme. The poem should say what we want it to say – rhyme is an extra.

   (See Workshop 9, 'The Robin', on p. 50.)

Rhythm

All poetry has some sort of rhythm – which is not to say that it necessarily has a regular thumping rhythm; sometimes an irregular, subtle rhythm or cadence is much more suited to the mood of a poem.

Riddles

A great tradition spanning *The Exeter Book* (Old English poetry) to the *Beano*. W. H. Auden memorably wrote that 'one of the elements of poetry is the riddle. You do not call a spade a spade.'

S

Shape poem

A poem whose words are laid out in a way that reflects the subject. Also called **Concrete poem**. (See Workshop 6, 'Waves'. See also www.shapepoems.co.uk)

Simile

A figure of speech in which one thing is said to be like (or as) another. See the example in the poem 'Writers' Workshop' on page 1: *Similes wait like actors in the wings.*

Stanza

The approved word to use for what is often referred to as a 'verse'!

T

Tanka

An extended form of haiku consisting of five lines and a total of 31 syllables, in the sequence 5, 7, 5, 7, 7. One of the great masters of tanka was Ki Tsurayuki. Here is a translation of one he wrote nearly a thousand years ago:

When I went to see,
That winter, my much loved girl,
The night wind blew
So cold against the river
That the water birds were crying.

It is a word picture similar to a haiku but its extended form means it can also have some story element.

Thin poem

One or two words per line. Set an arbitrary limit and stick to it. (See also **List poem**.)

U

Understanding

'But what does it *mean*?' Sometimes you cannot completely explain the meaning of a poem. That's part of the point of poetry – it has meanings behind and beyond its initial meaning. Sometimes just let a poem wash over you – don't try to understand it, just enjoy the sounds, the mood. The understanding of it might creep up on you bit by bit over time.

V

Verse

Often used to mean stanza (as in 'the poem has four verses') but properly used to mean something slightly less than poetry. I write verse and sometimes I write poetry. Sometimes my writing has the higher attributes of poetry, sometimes it has the rhyme, rhythm etc. associated with poetry, but it is of a lesser order.

Voice

Poems gain strength from being written in the poet's particular voice – the poet's own individual way of expressing himself or herself with words, images and language that are real and rooted in the poet's own life. (See Workshop 15, 'December'.) Allow children to use their everyday language within their poems. Poetry should not be kept on a pedestal.

W

Websites

There are many poetry websites you might find helpful. Here are just a few:

- Children's Poetry Bookshelf: www.childrenspoetrybooks.co.uk
- Poetry Society: www.poetrysociety.org.uk

- Poetryclass: www.poetryclass.net
- Foyle Young Poets of the Year Award: www.poetrysociety.org.uk/foyle
- The Poetry Archive: www.poetryarchive.org
- www.loc.gov/poetry/180/
- For writing games www.everybodywrites.org.uk/writing-games/primary/
- www.poetryzone.co.uk/
- Performance: http://performapoem.lgfl.org.uk
- www.poetrymagic.co.uk
- To hear popular children's poets reading their own poems go to www.poetryarchive.org/childrensarchive/home.do

Word games

Free the mind, focus on a skill or start the creative process by playing a word game. Excellent ideas can be found in *Word Games* by Sandy Brownjohn and Janet Whitaker (published by Hodder and Stoughton). See word game suggestions on http://www.everybodywrites.org.uk/writing-games/primary/

Writing frame

I've provided some for you; alternatively, you can make your own by taking a poem and blanking out a word (or words), a line, a simile. Do a line from time to time just as a quick activity. Take 'I wandered lonely as a cloud' and try as:

I _____ lonely as a _____.

Obviously a writing frame is just a starting point and a support – helpful sometimes, especially for the less confident.

If a frame proves in any way to be a restriction simply adapt or abandon it!

X

Excitement! Exultation! Exhilaration! Exclamations! (excusing myself from something beginning with X!).

Y

Yes! Yippee! and Yabbadabadoo! Feeling positive, feeling confident, having fun with words, writing a poem with . . .

Z

Zest and Zip and ZING!

Licensed to Thrill

A performance poem

Stand up tall.
Stand up proud.
Speak it *softly*.
Speak it **loud.**
Speak it clearly.
Take . . . your . . . time.
You'll be brilliant!
You'll be fine!
Do not fidget.
Do not mumble.
Stand still and strong.
Do not stumble.

Don't wibble or wobble or hop around.
Hold your head high. Don't stare at the ground.
Send your voice to the back of the room.
You can make it loud with a
Boom boom BOOM.
You can make it whispery, *soft* as a *sigh*.
Vary voice and volume. Use low and high.
No need to rush. No need to blush.
Just . . . have . . . fun.
You're as good as anyone.

And so . . .
Your performance is over.
What to do now?
Look at your audience
And
Take a bow.

Michaela Morgan

How to Teach Poetry Writing: Workshops for Ages 8–13, 2nd edn, Routledge © Michaela Morgan 2011

Workshop 1: Licensed to Thrill

Key concept
Performing poetry

This workshop is a starting point for young poets. Listening to verse and speaking it aloud is a vital step to appreciating and writing poetry.

The aim of this workshop is to add extra energy and enjoyment to the poetry class and to boost confidence.

The advice on performing poetry is given in the form of a performance poem. Children can use this verse as a springboard to their own performances and to writing their own performance poem.

In a playful way, awareness of punctuation and line-breaks is increased.

Read! speak! listen! enjoy!

- Enlarge and display the poem so that the whole class can see it. If you use a visualiser or an interactive whiteboard, keep a printed copy on display so that children can look at the poem repeatedly and in their own time.
- Show some poetry performance, e.g. use www.poetryarchive.org/ or www.poetryarchive.org/childrensarchive/home.do or performapoem.lgfl.org.uk
- Enjoy performing the poem. Read the poem aloud several times. Encourage children to work in pairs or groups, performing the poem.

Discuss

- Discuss the advice given on performing poetry. Is there more advice you could add?
- Look at punctuation. What hints does the punctuation give for performance? Demonstrate stopping for full stops, lingering (not too long) at a comma, pausing at ellipses etc.
- Look at line-breaks. Many of the lines are short and snappy but some lines run together (e.g. 'Hold your head high'. 'Don't stare at the ground'.) What effect should this have on the way the poem is read/performed?
- What other 'how-to-perform' clues can children find? Font? Boldness? Size? Choice of word?
- Are there any lines children particularly like? Why? Are there lines they would like to add or take away.

Write

Whole-class activity with teacher as scribe. Write a whole-class performance poem that gives instructions.

Some ideas to get started with are:

> what your mum/dad, friends/teacher says (do this/do that)
> how to score a goal (head it, kick it, lob it high . . .)
> how to train a pet
> how to get an idea

Move on to small group, pair, or independent work.

Hints for writing this performance poem:

- Note that instructions are usually short and snappy.
- They may be exclamations. Sit down! Stand up!
- Aim for economy of language.
- Don't be afraid to repeat a word or a phrase or to have a refrain:

  (e.g. My mum says 'tidy up'.
  My mum says 'read that book'.
  My mum says 'I've lost my key'.
  My mum says 'I'll kiss your knee'.)

- Performance poems often rhyme – but they don't have to.
- If you want to find extra rhymes use a good rhyming dictionary.
- If you can't find a rhyme you can re-order your line so that the last line rhymes more easily, you can leave it out, you can change the word.
- At the revision stage, look at cutting lines out or rearranging them for better effect.
- Look at line-breaks and punctuation. Will it give your readers a clue about how you want them to read the poem?

Perform! discuss! enjoy! applaud!

Put on a performance for the class or school. Performances can be recorded and uploaded to the Perform a Poem website. Hints for doing this are given on the website http://performapoem.lgfl.org.uk. This is an e-safe site founded by Michael Rosen.

Read on

Read other performance poems in a variety of styles and voices. Details of some collections of performance poems are given in the Bibliography on p. 97.

Follow-up

- Read a poem out to your class on a daily basis.
- A poem can be very short – so you WILL have the time.
- No discussion need be involved – just read it out and enjoy it.
- Check out competitions, e.g. the BBC ran the Off By Heart competition in which children were encouraged to learn a poem by heart and perform it. Schools can participate in competitions like this – or merely watch the programme http://www.bbc.co.uk/schools/teachers/offbyheart/
- Invite a poet to your school. This is possibly the best way to get your school buzzing with poetry (see p. 3 for advice).

Monday's Child

Monday's child is fair of face.

Tuesday's child is full of grace.

Wednesday's child is full of woe.

Thursday's child has far to go.

Friday's child is loving and giving.

Saturday's child works hard for a living

but the child that is born on the Sabbath day

is bonny and blythe and good and gay.

Anon. trad.

Workshop 2: Monday's Child

Read! speak! listen! enjoy!

- Display the poem so that the whole class can see it. If you use a visualiser or an interactive whiteboard, keep a printed copy on display so that children can look at the poem repeatedly and in their own time.
- Read the verse aloud. Different pupils read. Each reader could represent a day of the week.

Discuss

- Who wrote this poem? How old do you think it is? Did you already know it? Point out how much poetry we know without realising it, e.g. nursery rhymes and the oral tradition, jingles and songs...
- What clues can you find to the age of the poem? (subject matter, style, form, words used, anonymous author, traditional).
- Vocabulary: some of the words used in this verse are localised, antiquated or have changed their meaning over the years. Explain *Sabbath* ('Sunday' – or 'Saturday' in the Jewish tradition, but this verse is probably Scots or northern English), *bonny* ('good-looking', 'beautiful'), *gay* ('happy', 'light-hearted' – this is the original meaning of gay, which is now changing its meaning). Some of these words are still in current use in different parts of the country and in different communities.
- Can you think of any other words that have changed meaning over the years? *Wicked* is one perhaps? Can you think of any other words for *good-looking* and *happy* that are specific to certain localities?
- Discuss the form of this verse. It is in rhyming couplets. Identify the couplets and the rhyme scheme.
- Find examples of alliteration.

Analyse model

- The verse goes through the days of the week in turn, has a regular rhythm (beat it out) and rhyme scheme and is easily memorable.
- Discuss the use of a description like *fair of face*. Why would the verse be less effective if the line was 'Monday's child is pretty'?

Write

- **Whole-class activity: write a poem modelled on this one.**
  - Teacher as scribe, taking suggestions from the class and modelling the process of brainstorming, note-jotting, rough writing, choosing, changing...
  - In the class poem, aim to use the language of today – write a modern-day version.
  - Encourage the use of dictionary and thesaurus to find alternative words.
  - Here's one idea:

  Monday's child plays in the rain.
  Tuesday's child is such a pain.
  Wednesday's child is very cheeky.
  Thursday's child is somewhat sneaky.
  Friday's child is speedy and sporty.
  Saturday's child is rather naughty
  but the child that is born on the Sabbath day
  is as bad as the rest. It's true. OK!

- **Move on to independent work.**
  - Children can move on to writing their own individual poems based on the model and the whole-class poem.
  - Children who need support for this activity can be given a writing frame – with as many gaps in it as you feel appropriate. You may include some rhymes to help out:

  Monday's child stays in bed

  _____

  Wednesday's child is lazy too

  _____

  Friday's child screams and screams

  _____

  but the child that is born on the Sabbath day

  _____

  Rhymes: has a pain in the head/turns bright red/cries boo hoo/scoffs bowls of stew/loves ice-creams/has bad dreams/is the best of all – or so I say!/ no way/today/Hey! Hey!

Perform! discuss! enjoy! applaud!

Plenary and revision/redrafting

- Read out and comment on particularly good choices of words.
- Make the point that poems are worked and reworked. Can anyone suggest improvements or alternatives?
- Incorporate revisions.
- Ask children to write out or key in their lines, with revisions incorporated.
- Present as a collection or a display. You could also record or film the performance (see p. 3).

Possibilities for follow-up and cross-curricular links

- Look at the poem 'Mama Dot' by Fred D'Aguiar. This Guyanan-born writer has used what was a light-hearted days of the week framework to make a deeper poem. The poem tells the story of those who were taken from their homes and sold into slavery.

Mama Dot

Born on a Sunday
in the kingdom of
Ashante
Sold on a Monday
into slavery
Ran away on Tuesday
'cause she born free
Lost a foot on
Wednesday
when they catch she
Worked all Thursday
till her hair grey
Dropped on a Friday
when they burned she
Freed on a Saturday
in a new century

Fred D'Aguiar

- Compare the two poems.
- Display the poems so that the whole class can see them. If you use a visualiser or an interactive whiteboard, keep a printed copy on display so that children can look at the poems repeatedly and in their own time.
  - D'Aguiar's poem is also in couplets. Find the rhymes. Point out that the poet uses half-rhyme or near-rhyme as well as full rhyme.
  - It also goes through the days of the week. The poet uses this as a way of telling a life story: the days of the week are metaphorical, not literal, days.
  - The original 'Monday's Child' verse uses words that are rooted in a particular time, place and culture. D'Aguiar's poem is rooted in his tradition, history, language and culture.

- D'Aguiar's poem is written in a particular 'voice'. It sounds as if the story is being told to us by someone who understands, who 'speaks the same language'. This directness adds to its power, making it more memorable. If the poet had used more formal language and a more complex form, what effect would this have?

● Simply reading and enjoying the poem is enough but some children could move on to try writing a life-story poem on D'Aguiar's model. It could tell their own life story.

● Ask the children to make notes of milestones in their lives (e.g. born, walked, went to school, found a friend, learned to write, wrote this poem). Then turn their memories into a Days of the Week poem.

● Alternatively the children could use the life story of a specific historical figure (e.g. Anne Boleyn) or a representative historical figure such as a Roman, Viking, soldier etc.

● Link with History – e.g. history of slavery.

The Day the Zoo Escaped

The day the zoo escaped...

the zebras zipped out quickly,
the snakes slid out slickly,

the lions marched out proudly,
the hyenas laughed out loudly,

the mice skipped out lightly,
the parrots flew out brightly,

but the hippopotomus,
stubbornly,

just stayed where it was.

Michaela Morgan and Sue Palmer

How to Teach Poetry Writing: Workshops for Ages 8–13, 2nd edn, Routledge © Michaela Morgan 2011

Workshop 3: The Day the Zoo Escaped

Read! speak! listen! enjoy!

- Display the poem so that the whole class can see it. If you use a visualiser or an interactive whiteboard, keep a printed copy on display so that children can look at the poem repeatedly and in their own time.
- Read the verse aloud. Different pupils read, either individually or in groups.
- Encourage reading with expression – a different voice for *loudly, proudly, skipped, marched,* etc.
- Enjoy!

Discuss

- What form does this poem take? Does it rhyme? (Apart from the introductory line and the final line, the poem is written in rhyming couplets. Find the couplets.)
- Can you find any alliteration in the poem?

Analyse model

Consider and discuss the choice of words. Emphasise the range of synonyms for *went* or *walked*.

Write

- **Whole-class activity: revise and redraft the poem.**
  - Using the writing frame provided at the end of this workshop and acting as scribe, substitute more vigorous verbs for *went* and a variety of adverbs for *quickly*. The words do not have to rhyme, but they can if you wish. You could write the main body of the poem in couplets.
  - Make a list of words you might consider using. Use a dictionary and thesaurus to find synonyms for *walked, went* and *quickly*. (Some helpful words: *slithered, slid,*

rushed, charged, climbed, clambered, crept, scuttled, tiptoed, hurried, hopped, wandered, inched, scurried, shuffled, chased, ran; cheekily, scarily, creepily, bouncily, happily, sheepishly, sluggishly, slothfully, lazily, sleepily, rapidly, racily, sneakily, snakily, shakily, hastily.)

- **Independent work: write a poem based on the same model.**
  - Animals you might suggest using: wolves, eagles, tigers, bears, crocodiles, snakes, bats, wildcats, hippos, elephants, slugs, snakes, tortoises, etc.
  - You can substitute *slowly* (and synonyms for *slowly*) for *quickly*.

Perform! discuss! enjoy! applaud!

Plenary and revision/redrafting

- Read out and comment on particularly good choices of words.
- Make the point that poems are worked and reworked. Can anyone suggest improvements or alternatives?
- Incorporate revisions.
- Ask children to write or type out their lines – with revisions incorporated.
- Present as a collection or display. You could also record the performance (see p. 3).

Possibilities for follow-up and cross-curricular links

Write a poem using an adverb at the beginning, rather than the end, of each line:

Quietly the . . .

Silently the . . .

Brightly the . . .

(As in the James Reeves poem: 'Slowly the tide creeps up the sand'.)

- Link with PE and Movement. Make the movements described in the poem.
- Link with Citizenship – discussion of zoos and keeping animals in captivity.

Writing frame

Revise! Redraft! Improve!

The Day the Zoo Escaped

The day the zoo escaped...

the monkeys went out quickly,

the spiders went out quickly,

the tigers went out quickly,

the rabbits went out quickly,

the rats went out quickly,

the cheetah went out quickly,

but the sloth,

    sleepily,

        just hung around.

How to Teach Poetry Writing: Workshops for Ages 8–13, 2nd edn, Routledge © Michaela Morgan 2011

Haiku

1

Over the doorway
The ivy creeps in the light
Of evening's moon.

Matsuo Basho 1644–94

2

The grasshopper's cry
Does not reveal how very
Soon they are to die.

Matsuo Basho 1644–94

3

Beat This!

Every word counts
in a Japanese haiku
Try one for yourself!

Michaela Morgan

4

Taking Flight

Haiku haiku hai
haiku haiku haiku ku
first haiku of spring!

Michaela Morgan

5

A Splashing Time!

Splattering rain drops
Puddles grow into small ponds
Hopeful ducks arrive.

Michaela Morgan

How to Teach Poetry Writing: Workshops for Ages 8–13, 2nd edn, Routledge © Michaela Morgan 2011

Workshop 4: Every Word Counts

Read! speak! listen! enjoy!

- Display the poems so that the whole class can see them. If you use a visualiser or an interactive whiteboard, keep a printed copy on display so that children can look at the poem repeatedly and in their own time.
- Read the poems aloud several times. Different pupils read.
- Discuss the best ways of reading these. Taking your time to read the traditional haiku is essential – otherwise one gulp and it's gone. This will encourage children to perform their own work with care.
- With the two traditional haiku, read slowly and allow words to linger in the air. The lighthearted ones need a more throwaway style of performance. A group can read 'Taking Flight', making it sound like a cuckoo call in spring.
- Enjoy!

Discuss

- What do you notice about these poems? Ensure that the children realise that each set of three lines is a separate and individual poem.
- The length of the poems – they are very short. A haiku is just three lines long.
- The lack of rhyme. A poem has carefully chosen words – sometimes the words are chosen to rhyme, sometimes they are chosen for their meaning, sometimes for their sound/music or alliteration. In this case, they have been chosen for their meaning and for the number of syllables in each word.
- Remind the children what a syllable is. Practise counting beats by tapping out the children's names or very familiar words. Clap the beats to *Tom, Kerry, playground, December.*
- Count the beats in the words of the model poems. Mark the syllables in each word. Explain that a haiku is an old Japanese form of verse that always has five syllables in the first line, seven syllables in the second and five syllables in the last line.
- Haiku are usually snapshot word pictures that try to capture a moment in time.

- They encourage the writer to choose words carefully, to search for alternative words and be aware of syllables. They encourage writing with care – every word counts. Unnecessary words can be deleted (this is good practice for all poetry writing).

Analyse models

- The traditional Japanese models both describe nature and a particular time. The final line of a haiku often offers a sense of conclusion.
- Modern haiku is often more playful than traditional Japanese haiku, but still preserves the syllable count and the three-line form.
- Traditional haiku offers a calm, thoughtful mood. How does it achieve this? (By lack of pounding rhythm and rhyme, which would increase pace and take away from the contemplative quality of the poem.)
- Notice in haiku 1 that the definite article (*the*) before *evening's* has been omitted. Why? Comment on how often poetry is trimmed down to its essentials. A poet will revise a poem and delete.
- Notice the line endings in haiku 2. A poet chooses carefully where to start and end each line. Why has the poet ended the lines where he has?
- The three modern examples have added a title. The title does not just repeat the content of the verse – it tries to add something to it.

Write

- **Whole-class activity: write a haiku.**
  - Teacher as scribe.
  - Encourage the use of dictionary and thesaurus to find alternative words.
  - Subjects might include: a view out of the window (a word picture of something seen); a season; an animal or bird; a type of weather. Select a subject and gather words and ideas. What could you say about the subject?
  - Rough-draft the first line. Then reduce or extend it to the right number of syllables. You may have to add a word or take words away. You may have to change the line-breaks. You may have to revise vocabulary, finding alternative words with different syllable counts.
  - Demonstrate crossing out, reading out, checking and changing as part of the writing process. Encourage syllable counting and careful word choice. Encourage the finding of a title – one that does not simply repeat the subject of the poem but somehow adds to it.
- **Move on to independent work.** Children's haiku can be linked thematically – each taking a month to make a haiku calendar or each taking a colour to make a haiku rainbow.

Perform! discuss! enjoy! applaud!

Plenary and revision/redrafting

- Read out and comment on particularly good choices of words.
- Make the point that poems are worked and reworked. Can anyone suggest improvements or alternatives?
- Incorporate revisions.
- Ask children to write or key in their lines – with revisions incorporated.
- Present as a collection or display. You could also record the performance (see p. 3).

Possibilities for follow-up and cross-curricular links

- Read more haiku. Study the work of Basho, the exemplar of haiku poets. Discuss his work, comparing the poems to each other and picking out the familiar features in the work. Copy out and present a collection of these Japanese poems from the sixteenth century.
- Art or ICT links: copy out in Japanese style or word-process and import images.
- Science: write haiku dealing with weather, animals etc.
- Extend the writing of haiku into the writing of renga (a series of linked haiku); tanka (five lines in all, starting with five syllables in line one, then seven syllables in line two, five syllables in line three, and seven syllables each in lines four and five); and Ngu Utu (alternating lines of five and seven syllables in a poem of any length, ending with two rhymes of seven syllables).
- Link with current topic being studied by writing a haiku about it.

Kennings

Fin Flapper

Staring eyes
fair prize
golden darter
good gobbler
chase player
fast forgetter
flake eater
fin flapper.

Hill Hopper

Scratch scritcher
nose twitcher
thumb licker
bowl kicker
carrot cruncher
lettuce muncher
straw robber
tail bobber.

Guess what?

Round facer
no smiler
still stander
two hander
night friendly
heart beater
time keeper
sudden shrieker.

Michaela Morgan

How to Teach Poetry Writing: Workshops for Ages 8–13, 2nd edn, Routledge © Michaela Morgan 2011

Workshop 5: Fin Flapper

Key concepts

Kennings
Language choice and control
Creating new words

Read! speak! listen! enjoy!

- Display the poems so that the whole class can see them. If you use a visualiser or an interactive whiteboard, keep a printed copy on display so that children can look at the poem repeatedly and in their own time.
- Read the kennings aloud several times. Different pupils read. Group reads.
- Readers try to guess the answer to the riddle 'Guess what?' (an alarm clock), 'Fin Flapper' (a goldfish), 'Hill Hopper' (a rabbit).
- Enjoy!

Discuss

- This kind of poem is called a kenning. Discuss the form of the poem.
- Kennings use a descriptive technique in which you avoid actually stating the name of the thing you are describing. Instead you use a compound, usually two-word, description of it; often you use a series of such descriptions. A historical example would be *sharp stabber* (knife). More current examples include *medicine man* (doctor), *ice box* (fridge) or *ankle biter* (baby).
- Alliteration is commonly used in kennings.
- In Anglo-Saxon storytelling and verse you will find kennings. (See 'Possibilities for follow-up and cross-curricular links' below.)
- The length of the poems – kennings can be very short.
- The example poems rhyme, but kennings do not have to rhyme.

Analyse models

- How many words on a line?
- Other reasons behind the choice of words: the poet builds a mental picture of the thing he or she is describing, often leaving the most obvious clues till last. Thus a kenning can have elements of a riddle.

Write

- **Whole-class activity: write a kenning describing animals and everyday objects.**
  - Teacher as scribe.
  - Subjects might include: 'Tiger', 'Cat', 'Dog', 'Clock', 'Vacuum cleaner', 'Fridge', 'Pencil case'.
  - Think of the item you are describing and jot down the attributes attached to it.
  - Leave the most obvious ones (such as the stripes on a tiger) till last – or omit them.
  - Find two-word descriptions. So instead of saying *fierce and hungry tiger*, write *fierce feeder*.
  - You can use alliteration and rhyme but these are not necessary.
- **Move on to independent work.** Pupils write a kenning, but leave out the last line (naming the subject) and see if the class can guess it.

Perform! discuss! enjoy! applaud!

Plenary and revision/redrafting

- Read out and guess the subjects. Comment on particularly good choices of words.
- Make the point that poems are worked and reworked. Can anyone suggest improvements or alternatives?
- Incorporate revisions.
- Ask children to write out or key in their lines – with revisions incorporated.
- Present as a collection or display. You could also record the performance (see p. 3).

Possibilities for follow-up and cross-curricular links

- Links can be made with other topics in the curriculum – e.g. for Geography write a River kenning or a Volcano kenning.
- History: take a historic artefact (or a photo or illustration) and write a kenning describing that object. Items used as stimulus could be pictures of an Egyptian mummy, a gas mask, a Viking sword.
- Links can be made with riddles. Here is an example of an Anglo-Saxon riddle. Invite pupils to guess the answer (probably ice).

An Anglo-Saxon Riddle

The wave, over the wave, a
weird thing I saw,
through-wrought, and
wonderfully ornate:
a wonder on the wave –
water became bone.

Anon.

Waves

Big waves
small waves

sneaking to the shore waves

waves that CRASH!

waves that ROAR

waves that SPLASH

waves that inch towards the shore

wave that whispers soft and sighs

beats

retreats

and waves

goodbye

Workshop 6: Waves

Read! speak! listen! enjoy!

- Display the poem so that the whole class can see it. If you use a visualiser or an interactive whiteboard, keep a printed copy on display so that children can look at the poem repeatedly and in their own time.
- Read the poem aloud several times. Different pupils read – with expression, pace and volume appropriate to the words. Group reads.
- Look at the poem. It is in the shape of the thing it is describing.
- Enjoy!

Discuss

- This kind of poem is called a shape poem (or a concrete poem). The layout of the words represents the subject of the poem. A shape poem is always specially shaped to represent the subject, e.g. a shape poem about a banana will be banana-shaped.
- This poem also features calligrams. The formation of the letters – or the font used – represents the subject.
- This poem rhymes, but a shape poem does not have to rhyme – most do not. To see a wider range of shape poems see *The Works: Every kind of poem you will ever need for the Literacy Hour*, published by Macmillan, or go to www.shapepoems.co.uk

Analyse model

- Look at the language. Find examples of: onomatopoeia, alliteration, word play.
- Word play: in poetry one word may have more than one level of meaning. In this poem *beat* has several meanings ('to make a retreat', 'to defeat', 'to pound', 'to have a regular rhythmic movement or sound'). *Wave* also has more than one meaning – as a noun meaning 'a ridge of water that curls and breaks' and as a verb meaning 'to move one's hand to and fro in greeting'.
- Other reasons behind the choice of words: the poet builds a picture of the thing she is describing.

Write

- **Whole-class activity: write a shape poem.**
  - Teacher as scribe, taking suggestions from the class – modelling the process of brainstorming, note-jotting, choosing, changing, reading back, looking, listening, changing.
  - Subjects might include: a worm, a snake, rain, a spider's web, a hedgehog, an octopus, a flower, a cloud, a tree, a dinosaur.
  - First gather your thoughts about the subject. What would you want to say about a snake? How does it move? What sound does it make? etc. Brainstorm and gather words (*slither, slide, hiss, sneak...*). Use a dictionary, thesaurus and rhyming dictionary as appropriate. Think of words you can represent in shapes (*coil, twist, turn, loop...*). Then arrange your words in the shape of a snake or snakes.
  - Delete unnecessary words. Note that in the model poem the poet does not say *Waves can be big, sometimes they roar... they splash all over* and so on.
  - Reorder the words for best effect.
  - You can use alliteration, onomatopoeia, similes, word play (*the snake snakes around*) etc.
  - Rhyme is an option but not a necessity.
- **Move on to independent work.** Pupils write shape poems using ideas of their own or from the whole-class session.

Perform! discuss! enjoy! applaud!

- Read out and show the poems. Comment on particularly good choices of words.
- Make the point that poems are worked and reworked. Can anyone suggest improvements or alternatives? Are there words that could be cut out? Descriptions that could be added?
- Incorporate revisions.
- Ask children to write out their lines – with revisions incorporated.
- Present as a collection or display. You could also record the performance (see p. 3).

Possibilities for follow-up and cross-curricular links

Art and Literature: calligrams: collect synonyms and represent each word calligrammatically to convey the shades of meaning, e.g. said, **BELLOWED**, *whispered*, *shrieeeeeekd*.

(See also www.shapepoems.co.uk)

On and On

Is a well-wisher
    someone
who wishes at a well?

Is a bad speller
    one
who casts a wicked spell?

Is a shop lifter
    a giant
who goes around lifting shops?

Is a pop singer
    someone
who sings and then pops?

Is a fly fisherman
    an angler
who fishes for flies?

Is an eye-opener
    a gadget
for opening eyes?

Is a night nurse
    a nurse
who looks after the night?

Who puts it to bed
    and then
turns off the light?

Is a big spender
    a spendthrift
who is exceedingly big?

Is a pig farmer
    really
a land-owning pig?

Does a baby-sitter
    really
sit on tiny tots?

Is a pot-holer
    a gunman
who shoots holes in pots?

Roger McGough

Workshop 7: Further On

Read! speak! listen! enjoy!

- Display the poem so that the whole class can see it. If you use a visualiser or an interactive whiteboard, keep a printed copy on display so that children can look at the poem repeatedly and in their own time.
- Read the poem aloud and look at it.
- Enjoy!

Discuss

- This poem plays with language. It encourages a greater awareness of the language we use. This awareness is essential for development of an appreciation of poetry and an ability to write it. It is also fun!
- Word play in poetry – one word may have more than one level of meaning. Look at the examples in the poem and, in whole-class session, brainstorm some new ideas (compound words are a great resource for this). Here are some examples to get you started: hot dog, light switch, lighthouse, paper boy, pencil case, friendship, traffic jam.
- When the class have got the idea, they can move off to work alone, in pairs or in groups, to see how many more funny examples they can come up with.
- Gather together to share ideas.

Write

- Children can write their poem in pairs or alone, or you could bring the whole thing together in a class poem.
- It can rhyme (as in the example) or it could be an un-rhyming list – which is easier to do!

Perform! discuss! enjoy! applaud!

- Read out and show the poems. Comment on particularly good choices of words.
- Make the point that poems are worked and reworked. Can anyone suggest improvements or alternatives? Are there words that could be cut out? Are there words or stanzas that could be re-ordered and revised?
- Incorporate revisions.
- Ask children to write out or key in their poems – with revisions incorporated.

Possibilities for follow-up and cross-curricular links

- Present as a performance or display. You could also record or film the performance.
- For links with Art, use the poem to inspire some illustrations.
- ICT. Use word-processing skills to preserve and present the poem. Keying in a poem provides a good opportunity for revising line-breaks, presentation etc.

Example of a class poem. Here is a class poem that was made in a writing workshop with Y4. We chose to use rhyme (largely because I was involved and I can't help it!) but it would also work well as an un-rhymed list.

Further On

Is a playground
a ground
that likes playing around?

Is a sound idea
really
made out of sound?

Is a street dancer
a happy dancing street?

Is a ship-wreck
a ship
that is not very neat?

Is a butterfly
a fly
made out of butter?

Is a see-saw
really
a sharp sea cutter?

Is a football
a ball
made out of feet?

Is a beat box
a box
with a really good beat?

Is wrapping paper
paper
that likes to RAP?

Is a cat flap
a worried cat
all in a flap?

Is a bouncy ball
a dance
where people jump, jump, JUMP?

Is a monkey
a key
made out of a monk?

Is a chatterbox
a box
that likes to chatter?

A person
who naps on kids ...
Is that a kidnapper?

Is a rock climber
a rock
who likes to climb?

Is a sausage roll
a sausage
who rolls around all the time?

Is seaweed
the sea
that has just weed?

Is a scatter brain
a farmer
who scatters brains like seed?

*By Y4 Colwall Primary School including teacher
and teaching assistant and Michaela Morgan*

Space Rap

(Chorus): Say oh oh (oh oh)
Say Solar System
Say oh oh (oh oh)
On a rappin' mission (on a rappin' mission).
Planet number one is Mercury
And this is known through all the galaxy.
It's hot, it's hot, like a steaming pot.
So close to the Sun you'd toast like a bun
So living there would not be fun!

(Chorus)

The planet Venus is hotter still.
If you lived there you would be ill.
A place of gas and acid rain
Living there would be a pain!

(Chorus)

The planet Earth is number three.
The green is the land, the blue is the sea.
The average temperature is twenty-two.
We live here and that is true!

(Chorus)

Planet number four is the red one, Mars.
The name is famous – it's on chocolate bars.
It's a planet that has its own volcanoes.
It may have life there but nobody knows.

(Chorus)

Planet number five is Jupiter.
It's got a big hole, it'll make your mind stir.
It's the biggest planet of them all
Too big to use as – a football.

(Chorus)

Planet number six is called Saturn.
It orbits slowly but boy can it turn!
Saturn is a planet with icy rings
And in outer space it's one of the most colourful things.

(Chorus)

Planet number seven is Uranus.
If you landed there you would be famous.
It's minus two-hundred-and-ten degrees.
It's even got its very own seas.

(Chorus)

Neptune is planet eight.
It's always ready to rotate.
It's got a cloud by the name of Scooter.
It has a very nice blueish colour.

(Chorus)

Planet number nine is called Pluto.
It's made from ice and rock – so
the temperature is minus two-hundred-and-thirty degrees
Not like our planet – too cold for trees!

(Chorus)

Planet X is the unknown one.
As far as we know it's furthest from the Sun.
Some think it's there. Some think it's not.
Until we know for sure, that's nine we've got.

(Chorus): Say oh oh (oh oh)
Say Solar System
Say oh oh (oh oh)
On a rappin' mission (on a rappin' mission).

By a group of children in a Leicestershire school,
based on 'Solar System' by Jimmy Grey

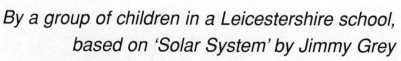

Workshop 8: Space Rap

Read! speak! listen! enjoy!

- Display the poem so that the whole class can see it. If you use a visualiser or an interactive whiteboard, keep a printed copy on display so that children can look at the poem repeatedly and in their own time.
- Read the poem aloud several times with expression, pace and volume as appropriate. Different pupils read. Group reads.
- Enjoy!

Discuss

- Who wrote this poem? (It is a collaborative poem. The class enjoyed a rap by Jimmy Grey from *Rap with Rosen*, published by Longman. All the class thought of a chorus and gathered ideas. Then groups chose a planet and wrote a stanza about that planet. They incorporated the information they had gathered in their study of the solar system.)
- Discuss subject matter, style, words used, form.
- Raps always rhyme and it's sometimes hard to find a rhyme. What can you do when this happens?
  - Rearrange the line so it ends with another word.
  - Choose another word to replace the one that is hard to rhyme with.
  - Use a rhyming dictionary.
- Sometimes poets make up words but they do this on purpose – it's easy when rhyming to be silly by accident!
- This rap has a chorus, which is quite simple but holds the whole poem together and is fun to join in with.

Analyse model

As this is a rap, it has an emphatic rhythm and rhyme scheme and maintains a fast pace. Look at rhyme scheme in the model and beat out the rhythm.

Find the places where the rhythm needs tightening. Revise the poem and improve it where you can.

Write

- Whole-class activity: make up a chorus.
  - Take the topic you are currently working on and try to make up a refrain or chorus. Topic possibilities: Light, The Tudors, The Romans, Our School, Myself.
  - Teacher as scribe.
  - Make up a chorus, e.g. for the six wives of Henry VIII (Tudors): divorced, beheaded, died, divorced, beheaded, survived.
  - Encourage the use of a dictionary, thesaurus and rhyming dictionary.
  - Groups or individuals write a stanza of the class-topic rap, e.g. for the Romans: We build roads straight and long/We fought foes and won – we're strong...
- **Move on to independent work.** Pupils can write raps using ideas of their own or from the whole-class session.

Perform! discuss! enjoy! applaud!

- Get together again and perform the chorus, then listen to each stanza being performed. Applaud!
- Emphasise that these are drafts. Consider revisions. Are there any places where the rhythm or the rhyme could be improved? Scribe the whole piece working in revisions sensitively.
- Ask children to write or type out their lines – with revisions incorporated.

Possibilities for follow-up and cross-curricular links

Science: introduction to the planets.
Music: use percussion to add music to the performance.
Listen to other music about the planets (e.g. *The Planets* Suite by Holst).

- A public performance (e.g. assembly) of the rap.
- Art: write the rap up for a display. Use lettering to stress volume and subject, e.g. *rap it BIG* and *rap it **bold***.
- Collect other raps to add to this display or anthology.
- Make a recording of the children rapping.
- Rap your spelling lists!
- Ask groups to find another rap they like. Perform it, and then explain what they like about that particular rap.
- Retell a legend, myth, or tale in a rap.

The Robin

I tried to write a poem today,
I tried to make it rhyme,
I tried to get the meaning right
But every single time
I thought I'd got the hang of it,
I thought I'd got it right,
I found I couldn't think of a word
To rhyme with bird
Or, that is, robin.

I didn't want to say
I saw a robin.
It was bobbing
Along and sobbing.
Because it wasn't.

So I started again.

Once, last winter, in the snow,
I was out in the garden
At the bird table,
When I turned round
And saw on the path beside me
A robin.

It was so close
I could have touched it.
It took my breath away.

I have never forgotten
The red of it
And the white snow falling.

June Crebbin

How to Teach Poetry Writing: Workshops for Ages 8–13, 2nd edn, Routledge © Michaela Morgan 2011

Workshop 9: The Robin

Speaking and listening

- Display the poem so that the whole class can see it. If you use a visualiser or an interactive whiteboard, keep a printed copy on display so that children can look at the poem repeatedly and in their own time.
- Read the poem aloud to the class without them joining in. This is a poem for one voice rather than group participation.
- Point out that many poems have a bouncy rhythm and the opportunity to join in but some are quieter, more thoughtful, and you can read them aloud with one voice or to yourself. Point out that some poems rhyme but rhyme is not necessary.
- Check that everyone has understood the poem.
- What difference would it make to a poem about a robin if it had to rhyme? It would become bouncier; the mood would be lost. The poet might not have been able to capture what she felt and what she had seen. Emphasise again that rhyming is not essential to poetry. Rhyming is fun and is sometimes right for a poem, but if it stops you saying/writing what you want to say, if it makes you write nonsense by *mistake*, start again – this time without rhyme.
- Consider the layout of the poem. See how the poet alters the pace of the poem. She slows it down by leaving spaces. Look at the effect of 'So I started again' having space around it. Why is 'A robin' on a line all of its own? Notice how the length of the lines and the punctuation alter the pace and the effect of the poem.

Reading and writing

- As a whole class or in groups, take an object and try to capture it in a non-rhyming description. One 'poetic sentence' will be a good start. Objects could be anything that might mean something to the class (e.g. a well-worn teddy bear, a picture, a view out of the window, a favourite object. You could link to the topic you are studying, e.g. the Egyptians – use a picture of an impressive artefact).
- Brainstorm words and ideas and scribe them onto a flipchart or interactive whiteboard.

- Look at the lines you have scribed for the children and try out different word orders, line-breaks and different choices of words.

Further work and cross-curricular links

- Link this workshop with the senses and the following workshop, 'The Poem Hunt'.
- For Science, link with weather/seasons.
- Non-fiction research. Find facts on the robin or the article you have chosen as the subject of your poem. Some of this information can be used in the poem. Differentiate between the language and approach of non-fiction and poetry.

Workshop 10: The Poem Hunt

Key concept

The senses

This workshop does not start with the hearing or reading of a poem; it starts with an exploration.

- First, remind the children of the five senses: sight, hearing, smell, taste, touch.
- Compare the poet to an explorer. He or she uses all their senses and tries to look at the world with open eyes, all senses on the alert – as if they have newly discovered the world. (Re-read 'The Robin', p. 49 by June Crebbin, to emphasise this point).
- Go on a poem hunt to make poetic sentences. Take a clipboard or the worksheet out to the playground or around the school or use it on a school outing. Omit some senses if they are irrelevant to a particular exploration (e.g. to discourage tasting of inappropriate objects!) or if you feel the activity is too challenging for some. Smells are particularly challenging to capture and describe. An exploration of the school hall including a storage cupboard produced some excellent descriptions!
- You can add imagination to the list for some children (I imagine/I think/I feel/I dream) to try to capture mood.
- When the words and sentences have been captured, take the worksheets of rough notes back to the classroom to be rewritten and redrafted. Cutting out all unnecessary words and making changes will improve the description and make them more like a poem. It is important to do several whole-class redrafts to show the way. For example:

> *I see a tree*
> *it is bent*
> *like an old man*

becomes:

> *I see a tree, bent like an old man.*

> *I hear some other children*
> *whispering to each other*
> *like the wind*

becomes:

> *I hear children, whispering like the wind.*

> *I smell*
> *the air*
> *it's a nice fresh breeze*

becomes:

> *I smell the fresh breezy air.*

> *I touch a stone*
> *it is warm*
> *like a pet*

becomes:

> *I touch a stone, warm as a pet*
> or
> *I pet a stone, warm to my touch.*

- Now, or at a later date, ask each child to put all his or her 'poetic sentences' together to make a senses poem. Small changes can still be made to improve the poem. Words can be taken away or added:

> *I see a tree, bent like an old man.*
> *I hear children, whispering like the wind.*
> *I smell the fresh breezy air*
> *and touch a stone, warm as a pet.*

- Finally, think of a title.

Further work and cross-curricular links

- The young poets on their poem hunt have been like explorers, looking around a place carefully. A link with this theme of exploration could lead to work on famous explorers, Moon exploration etc.
- Link with Geography: make a map of the area explored (e.g. the playground).
- Science: link with work on the senses.
- ICT: key in poems. Use a digital camera to record images that accompany the descriptions and import these pictures.

Poem Hunt

I see a _____

it is [*describe it*] _____

it is like a_____ .

I hear a _____

it is [*describe it*] _____

it is like a_____ .

I smell a _____

it is [*describe it*] _____

it is like a_____ .

I touch a_____

it is [*describe it*] _____

it is like a_____ .

I Am a Baggy T-Shirt

I am a cheeky monkey, climbing and clambering.

I am a baggy T-shirt, hanging out.

I am a comfy sofa, relaxed, lounging.

I am the colour yellow, mellow and sunny.

I am a yellow pepper, fresh and cheerful.

I am a sunflower, waving in the sun.

I am a Rice Krispie, popping with fun!

By a group of children in an Essex school

How to Teach Poetry Writing: Workshops for Ages 8–13, 2nd edn, Routledge © Michaela Morgan 2011

Workshop 11: I Am a Baggy T-Shirt

Key concepts

Metaphor
Figurative language

Read! speak! listen! enjoy!

- Display the poem so that the whole class can see it. If you use a visualiser or an interactive whiteboard, keep a printed copy on display so that children can look at the poem repeatedly and in their own time.
- Read the poem aloud several times. Different pupils read. Group reads.
- Enjoy!

Discuss

- Who wrote this poem?
- How old do you think the poem is?
- What clues can you find to the age of the poem? (subject matter, style, words used, spellings, form).
- A poem has carefully chosen words – sometimes the words are chosen to rhyme, sometimes they are chosen for their meaning, sometimes for their sound/music or alliteration. In this case, apart from the final two lines, the words do not rhyme. Instead, what is special is the use of figurative language to conjure up mental pictures.
- Through the language in the poem we gain a picture of the person described. Are they tall or short? tense or relaxed? friendly? fun? serious? dark? blonde?
- The poem uses metaphor. When a writer uses a metaphor he or she makes a comparison but does not say one thing is *like* another; he or she says one thing *is* another, e.g. *She is pure poison.*

Analyse model

- Can you find any alliteration?
- Find the only example of a rhyme in the poem. Discuss the effectiveness of ending the poem with a rhyming couplet.

Write

- **Whole-class activity: write a description of a well-known character.**
  - Teacher as scribe, demonstrating the process of writing, thinking, crossing out and improving.
  - Subjects might include: a character in fiction or history, or a pop or film star.
  - Describe the person as some of the following: an animal, bird, fish; a plant or flower; an item of furniture; a vehicle; a colour; a food or drink; an item of clothing; a building.
  - Try to end the poem on a rhyming couplet.
- **Move on to independent work.** Pupils write poems describing themselves, their friends or 'mystery' characters.

Perform! discuss! enjoy! applaud!

- Read out and comment on particularly good choices of words. In the case of 'mystery' poems, guess who has been described.
- Remind the children of the definition of a metaphor. Which metaphors have they particularly enjoyed? Why?
- Make the point that poems are worked and reworked. Can anyone suggest improvements or alternatives?
- Incorporate revisions.
- Ask children to write out or key in their poems – with revisions incorporated.
- Present as a collection or as a display. You could also record or film the performance (see p. 3).

Possibilities for follow-up and cross-curricular links

- Take one of the metaphors used in the whole-class poem and develop it.
- Take a historical figure as the subject of a poetic description using metaphor.

The Sound Collector

A stranger called this morning
Dressed all in black and grey
Put every sound into a bag
And carried them away

The whistling of the kettle
The turning of the lock
The purring of the kitten
The ticking of the clock

The popping of the toaster
The crunching of the flakes
When you spread the marmalade
The scraping noise it makes

The hissing of the frying-pan
The ticking of the grill
The bubbling of the bathtub
As it starts to fill

The drumming of the raindrops
On the window pane
When you do the washing up
The gurgle of the drain

The crying of the baby
The squeaking of the chair
The swishing of the curtain
The creaking of the stair

A stranger called this morning
He didn't leave his name
Left us only silence
Life will never be the same.

Roger McGough

How to Teach Poetry Writing: Workshops for Ages 8–13, 2nd edn, Routledge © Michaela Morgan 2011

Workshop 12: The Sound Collector

Read! speak! listen! enjoy!

- Display the poem so that the whole class can see it. If you use a visualiser or an interactive whiteboard, keep a printed copy on display so that children can look at the poem repeatedly and in their own time.
- Read the poem aloud several times. Different pupils read. Group reads.
- Enjoy!

Discuss

- Who wrote this poem?
- How old do you think the poem is?
- What clues can you find to the age of the poem? (subject matter, style, words used, form).
- Onomatopoeia – words that demonstrate the sounds they are describing – is a feature of this poem (e.g. *whistling, popping*). How many examples of onomatopoeia can you find in the poem?

Analyse model

- Discuss the form of the poem. How many lines to a stanza? Does it rhyme? (quatrains with second and fourth lines rhyming; the rhyme scheme is *abcb*).
- A poem has carefully chosen words – sometimes the words are chosen to rhyme, sometimes they are chosen for their meaning, sometimes for their sound/music or alliteration. In this case, they have been chosen for their rhyme, rhythm and onomatopoeia.
- The poem tells a story. It is a narrative poem. The four-line stanza is the form used for traditional narrative poems – ballads.
- How would you describe the mood of this poem?

Write

- **Whole-class activity: add further stanzas to the poem.**
  - Can you suggest words to describe each sound, e.g. *glug* for *gurgle*. Write them on the model.
  - Read the poem again with some readers making the sounds (*hiss, pop, glug*) after the appropriate line.
  - Teacher as scribe.
  - Add further stanzas. Subjects might include: the telly, a sister on the phone, a mother's moan, a humming fridge, a whining brother, a grumbling gran, a computer game, a pet. (Some pupils will benefit from doing this as a group or in a pair rather than as an individual activity.)
- **Move on to independent work.**
  - Pupils write a poem, or a stanza of a poem, based on the model, but with the stranger stealing the noises from the school or playground. You can use the writing frame at the end of this workshop to help – *but feel free to modify the model if you need to.*
  - First think of the sounds of school (clock *ticking*, pencils *scritch-scratching*, paint *sploshing*, *shrieking* from the playground, *thumping* from the hall, *clattering* of cutlery...). Use a thesaurus, dictionary and rhyming dictionary as appropriate.
  - Words and ideas to help: *squeaking, creaking, scratching, door, floor, chalk, talk, pattering, sploshing, dripping, taps, hamster, books dropping, turning pages, shushing, bell ringing, singing, in the hall, hushing, screaming from the play-ground, piercing whistle, shriek, squeaking new shoes, drawer, quiet, creak, scratching, pencil, sudden, splosh, paint, humming computer, tapping of the keyboard, clicking of the mouse, squeaking of the felt tip, birds, outside.*

Perform! discuss! enjoy! applaud!

Plenary and revision/redrafting

- Read out and comment on particularly good choices of words.
- Make the point that poems are worked and reworked. Can anyone suggest improvements or alternatives?
- Incorporate revisions.
- Ask children to write or type out their lines – with revisions incorporated.
- Present as a collection or as a display. You could also record or film the performance (see p. 3).

Possibilities for follow-up and cross-curricular links

- Read other poems by Roger McGough.
- Collect examples of onomatopoeia from everyday language.
- Invent examples. For example, make up new onomatopoeic words to describe manu-factured products (a new cleaning liquid, glue, sweets, drinks, foods, etc.).
- Look at traditional ballads and other narrative poems. Read these aloud. Discuss and compare them.
- Science: discussion of sound. How sound travels on Earth/in space/under water.
- Music: use instruments or voices to replicate the sounds mentioned in the poems.

Writing frame

The School Sound Collector

A stranger called this morning
Dressed all in black and grey
Put every sound into a bag
And carried them away

The _turning_ of the _pages_ (a)
The _reciting_ of the _ages_ (b rhyme here)
The _beating_ of the _drum_ (c)
The _slurping_ of the _rum_ (b rhyme here)

The _____ of the _____
The _____ of the _____ (rhyme here)
The _____ of the _____
The _____ of the _____ (rhyme here)

A stranger called this morning
He didn't leave his name
Left us only silence
Life will never be the same.

How to Teach Poetry Writing: Workshops for Ages 8–13, 2nd edn, Routledge © Michaela Morgan 2011

Nocturnophobia

I am scared of the dark

Like a tree is nervous of autumn

Like a pencil is terrified of an eraser

Like a window is anxious about a football

Like a log is horrified by a chainsaw

Like a car is afraid of the crusher

I am scared of the dark.

By a group of children in an East Sussex school

How to Teach Poetry Writing: Workshops for Ages 8–13, 2nd edn, Routledge © Michaela Morgan 2011

Workshop 13: Nocturnophobia

Read! speak! listen! enjoy!

- Display the poem so that all the class can see it.
- Read the poem aloud several times. Different pupils read. Group reads.
- Enjoy!

Discuss

- Who wrote this poem? (It is a collaborative poem – with many children contributing a line to it.)
- The lack of rhyme. A poem has carefully chosen words – sometimes the words are chosen to rhyme, sometimes they are chosen for their meaning, sometimes for their sound/music or alliteration. In this case, the words have been chosen for their images – for their figurative language. The poem is in free verse. It has no rhymes but the language is still carefully chosen.
- The children have invented a word for their title. *Nocturne* is a reference to night and *phobia* is fear, so their title means 'fear of the night'. Poets sometimes invent new words or *portmanteau* terms – joining two words together to make a new word. There are many examples of this in Lewis Carroll's 'Jabberwocky'.

Analyse model

- Look at the form of this poem. It starts with the poets telling us something about themselves ('I am scared of the dark'). This is autobiographical detail.
- Then there are a number of comparisons made. These are similes – one thing is described as being like another. The similes help us to understand more fully what is being described. The feeling of being scared is described and the imagery used helps us to understand that feeling by putting the feeling into word pictures.
- At the end of the list of similes the poets repeat their first line.
- The poem is in free verse. It is not limited by rhyme or rhythm, although there is a rhythm and pattern to it.

- The things being described are inanimate objects (a tree, a log, a car) not people. But they are described as if they are people – with the feelings of people. The poets have used personification.

Write

- **Whole-class activity: write a poem based on the model.**
  - Teacher as scribe.
  - Start with *I am scared of...* Discuss and list synonyms for scared of *(terrified of/by, petrified of/by, nervous of, worried by, fearful of,* etc.). Encourage the use of a dictionary and thesaurus.
  - Continue the poem using similes and personification as in the model.
  - You can write other group poems varying the subject matter (*I am happy about...; I look forward to . . . ; I am hopeful about . . . ; I am fed up with . . .*).
- **Move on to independent work.**
  - Individual children can write their own poems. These poems can be connected into a sequence of poems describing feelings.
  - Pupils can make up their own titles. They can invent a word as the poets of the model poem did. Use an etymological dictionary to help.

Perform! discuss! enjoy! applaud!

Plenary and revision/redrafting

- Read out and comment on particularly good choices of words.
- Make the point that poems are worked and reworked. Can anyone suggest improvements or alternatives?
- Incorporate revisions.
- Ask children to write or type out their lines – with revisions incorporated.
- Present as a sequence on feelings. These poems are linked by their theme and form.
- Make a collection or display. You can record or film performances (see p. 3).

Possibilities for follow-up and cross-curricular links

- Collect and read other poems about fears and feelings.
- Link with PSHE and Citizenship – discussion of feelings.

Three

I met a miniature King
by the side of the road,
wearing a crown
and an ermine suit –
important, small,
plump as a natterjack toad,
Kneel! he shrieked, *Kneel for the King!*
CERTAINLY not, I said, *I'll do no such thing.*

I saw a Giantess,
tall as a tree.
You'll do for a new doll, she bellowed,
just the toy for me!
Into the box! Scream hard! Scream long!
I stared at her mad, pond eyes
then skipped away.
Dream on . . .

I bumped into Invisible Boy – *ouch!* –
at the edge of the field.
Give me a chocolate drop
said a voice.
What do you say?
Please.
So I did
then stared as it floated mid-air
and melted away.
These are three of the people I met yesterday.

Carol Ann Duffy

How to Teach Poetry Writing: Workshops for Ages 8–13, 2nd edn, Routledge © Michaela Morgan 2011

Workshop 14: Three

Read! speak! listen! enjoy!

- Display the poem so that the whole class can see it. If you use a visualiser or an interactive whiteboard, keep a printed copy on display so that children can look at the poem repeatedly and in their own time.
- Read the poem aloud several times. Different pupils read with appropriate expression, pace and volume. Group reads.
- Enjoy!

Discuss

- Who wrote this poem? Carol Ann Duffy is currently the Poet Laureate. Children can research the history of this post and previous laureates. Compare with later workshop ('The Charge of the Light Brigade', p. 82), which features the work of a much earlier laureate.
- How old do you think the poem is?
- What clues can you find to the age of the poem? (subject matter, style, words used, spellings, form).
- Rhyme. A poem has carefully chosen words – sometimes the words are chosen to rhyme, sometimes they are chosen for their meaning, sometimes for their sound/music or alliteration. This poem has an irregular use of rhyme. Find the rhymes.
- The poem also has an uneven number of lines; it combines free verse with the occasional rhyme. It is a contemporary poem – contemporary poems are often looser than traditional ones.

Analyse model

- This poem has a dreamlike fantasy feel to it. Each stanza starts with the narrator meeting a figure from a fantasy/myth/fairy tale. The poem illustrates the benefits of using your previous reading, experience and dreams when reading and writing.

- Language. Find alliteration. Find rhymes, including assonance and half-rhymes (*Scream long!* and *Dream on...*) and internal rhymes (*stared...mid-air*). Find synonyms for *said*.
- Discuss the description of the king. Pick out the descriptions you like.
  - Comment on the juxtaposition of *important* and *small* – is this unexpected? contradictory? What impression does it give of him?
  - Comment on the word *plump*. What other synonyms for *plump* can you suggest? What effect does each word have?
  - Discuss the comparison of the king with a toad. Point out that this is a simile – does it work?
- Look at the description of the eyes of the Giantess (*mad, pond eyes*). What does this description mean? Point out that this is a metaphor – her eyes are described as if they really are ponds. Think of what a pond is like (murky, perhaps deep, without reflection).
- Idioms. Comment on *I bumped into...* Point out that this is an idiomatic expression, but that here the poet has played with the words using the idiom as if it was literally true (*I bumped into Invisible Boy – ouch!*). The poet has also played with the cliché *Dream on...* Here it has two meanings ('No, I won't!' and 'I will carry on with my dreamy journey'). Poems often use word play. Think of other idiomatic expressions that you could play with by using them literally (e.g. *He laughed his head off; I kept an eye on my little sister; She asked me to lend a hand.*) Link with Workshop 7, 'Further On', p. 42.
- Look at the line-breaks. Why has the poet chosen to end the lines where she has?
  - In the third stanza, why is *So I did* on a line all by itself? (It gives the line emphasis and pause. Line-breaks tell us how to read the poem and pace our reading.)
  - In the first stanza, look at *Kneel! he shrieked, Kneel for the King!* – all on one line for a faster pace. The same applies to *Into the box! Scream hard! Scream long!* Keeping this all on one line makes for a quicker pace – a hint of frenzy.
  - Note that the poet does not always use full sentences. She uses an economical style. Discuss how *just the toy for me! Into the box!* is more dramatic than *You are just the toy for me. Get into this box.* Point out the economy of poetry – how poets cut out unnecessary words. Find other examples of this (*I saw a Giantess, tall as a tree*, not *I saw a Giantess. She was as tall as a tree*).
- Look at the punctuation in the poem. Note the clues it gives us about the tone, mood and pace.

Write

- **Whole-class activity: using a writing frame.**
  - Complete the writing frame at the end of the workshop.
  - Teacher as scribe, modelling the process of choosing words, changing one's mind, revising, cutting out unnecessary words, using rhymes or alliteration, making a comparison, etc.
- **Move on to independent work.** Pupils write their own stanza. Creatures met could be: a dragon, a knight, a hero, an angel, a witch, a monster, etc.

Perform! discuss! enjoy! applaud!

Plenary and revision/redrafting

- Read out and comment on particularly good choices of words, punctuation, line-breaks, word play, comparisons etc.
- Make the point that poems are worked and reworked. Can anyone suggest improvements or alternatives? Discuss improvements made and the effects they had.
- Incorporate revisions.
- Ask children to write or type out their lines – with revisions incorporated.
- Present as a collection or as a display. You could also record or film the performance (see p. 3).

Possibilities for follow-up and cross-curricular links

- Link the children's individual poems to make a series poem for performance.
- Turn the poem into a play script and perform.
- Link with work on fable and myth.
- Link with work on idioms. (See Appendix: 'Figuratively Speaking' and Workshop 7, 'Further On'.)
- History: write the poem using three characters from history as the characters met.
- Geography/Science: encounter three geological features (e.g. volcano/tidal wave, earthquake).

One

I met a (who/what did you meet? – someone/thing from a legend/myth/fairy tale)

(Where did you meet him/her/it?) _____

(Describe him/her/it) _____

_____

(What did he/she/it say?) _____

_____

(What did you say/do?) _____

_____

This is one of the people I met yesterday.

Now check this over.
Cut out unnecessary words.
Put in strong, carefully chosen words.
Check that your punctuation will give your reader clues as to
how to read this – where to pause, exclaim etc.
Look at your line-breaks.
Are there any changes you can make to improve your poem?

December

De snow, de sleet, de lack of heat,
De wishy-washy sunlight,
De lip turn blue, de cold, "ACHOO!"
De runny nose, de frostbite

De creakin' knee, de misery
De joint dem all rheumatic,
De icy bed, (de blanket dead)
De burs' pipe in de attic

De window a-shake, de glass near break,
De wind dat cut like razor
De wonderin' why you never buy
De window from dat double-glazer

De thick new coat, zip up to the throat,
De nose an' ears all pinky,
De weepin' sky, de clothes can't dry,
De days dem long an' inky.

De icy road, de heavy load,
De las' minute Christmas shoppin'
De cuss an' fret 'cause you feget
De ribbon an' de wrappin'.

De mud, de grime, de slush, de slime,
De place gloomy since November,
De sinkin' heart, is jus' de start, o'
De wintertime,
December.

Valerie Bloom

How to Teach Poetry Writing: Workshops for Ages 8–13, 2nd edn, Routledge © Michaela Morgan 2011

Workshop 15: December

Poems reflecting different cultures and voices
Internal rhyme
Comparison of different treatment of classic and contemporary themes

Read! speak! listen! enjoy!

- Display the poem so that the whole class can see it. If you use a visualiser or an interactive whiteboard, keep a printed copy on display so that children can look at the poem repeatedly and in their own time.
- Read the poem aloud several times. Different pupils read. Group reads.
- Enjoy!

Discuss

- Who wrote this poem?
- How old do you think the poem is? What clues can you find to its age? (subject matter, style, words used, spellings, form).
- Notice that the poet has used the voice, rhythm and accent of the Caribbean. Pick out examples of these.
- Form, rhyme and rhythm.
  - A poem has carefully chosen words – sometimes the words are chosen to rhyme, sometimes they are chosen for their meaning, sometimes for their sound/music or alliteration. This poem is in quatrains and has a lively rhythm. The pace is emphasised by the rhyme.
  - On lines 1 and 3 in each stanza, there are rhymes within the lines (internal rhymes). These increase the pace of the poem. Look at the last stanza. How does the poet slow the poem down to finish it?

Analyse model

- How does the poet make this poem sound so real and contemporary?
- Pick out and discuss particular lines and words you like. What gives them their appeal?
- Who do you think is speaking in this poem? Do the concerns with cold, rheumatism, etc. hint at a certain age? How would the poem differ if written from a child's perspective? if written by an Australian?

● Share and discuss 'November' by Thomas Hood (p. 73). This has provided a starting point for Valerie Bloom's poem. Point out the word play both poets have employed. Hood has played with *No* and Valerie Bloom has played with *De* so that both lead up to a play on the name of the month November or December. Can you think of word play on the names of other months. 'May' would work (In May you may...); 'March' might work (Marching to March); 'July' (In July you lie...).

Write

● **Whole-class activity: using a writing frame.**
  – Teacher as scribe, modelling the process of gathering thoughts, changing one's mind, searching for words, redrafting etc.
  – Complete the writing frame at the end of the workshop. Valerie Bloom has written about the unpleasantness of December. Think about the good things associated with December and complete the frame accordingly.
● **Move on to independent work.** Pupils write their own stanza about December. Some pupils could also try a poem about another month.

Perform! discuss! enjoy! applaud!

Plenary and revision/redrafting

● Read out and comment on particularly good choices of words.
● Make the point that poems are worked and reworked. Can anyone suggest improvements or alternatives?
● Incorporate revisions.
● Ask children to write out or key in their poems – with revisions incorporated.
● Present as a collection or as a display. You could also record or film the performance (see p. 3).

Possibilities for follow-up and cross-curricular links

● Read other poems about the seasons. Compile an anthology of poems on this subject.
● Valerie Bloom's poem has been modelled on a well-known poem by Thomas Hood. Poets usually read a lot of poetry and are inspired by the works of fellow poets, including poets from very different times and places.

November

No sun – no moon!
No morn – no noon –
No dawn – no dusk – no proper time of day –
No sky – no earthly view –
No distance looking blue –
No road – no street – no 't'other side the way' –
No end to any Row –
No indications where the Crescents go –
No top to any steeple –
No recognitions of familiar people –
No courtesies for showing 'em –
No knowing 'em –
No travelling at all – no locomotion –
No inkling of the way – no notion –
'No go' – by land or ocean –
No mail – no post –
No news from any foreign coast –
No Park – no Ring – no afternoon gentility –
No company – no nobility –
No warmth, no cheerfulness, no healthful ease,
No comfortable feel in any member –
No shade, no shine, no butterflies, no bees,
No fruits, no flowers, no leaves, no birds –
November!

Thomas Hood (1799–1845)

Enlarge Hood's poem and compare the two. Explain that Novembers were foggier in Thomas Hood's time! Both poems use a particular voice capturing a particular time and culture. Both employ informal language. Both have played with words.

- Practise performing 'November' by Thomas Hood and 'December' by Valerie Bloom. Then put together stanzas made by children to form a class poem to perform.
- Groups or individuals can take a month of the year and write a stanza about it. This can be put together to make the 'Poem of the Year'. Each month can be in a separate form and style, revisiting different styles of poetry encountered by the children, e.g. kennings, haiku, use of metaphor, use of personification etc.
- Topics: you could link the discussion of these poems to a discussion of weather, global warming, clean air and pollution. There are also links with Citizenship (the old and the cold) and with Science (insulation/heat/cold). Links can also be made with the topics of countries and weather.

December

De eyes a glow, the skies of _____

De shall we have a snow fight?

De toasty feet, the fire's _____

De starshine and de Moon _____

De frost all round, de slidey_____

De Christmas tills a'ringin'

De seasonal sights, de twinkly _____

De Christmas songs for _____

How to Teach Poetry Writing: Workshops for Ages 8–13, 2nd edn, Routledge © Michaela Morgan 2011

Hubble Bubble

From *Macbeth*

Thrice the brinded cat hath mew'd.
Thrice and once, the hedge-pig whin'd.
Harpier cries: 'tis time! 'tis time!

Round about the caldron go;
In the poison'd entrails throw.
Toad, that under cold stone,
Days and nights has thirty-one;
Swelter'd venom sleeping got,
Boil thou first i' the charmed pot!

Double, double toil and trouble;
Fire burn, and caldron bubble.

Fillet of a fenny snake,
In the caldron boil and bake;
Eye of newt, and toe of frog,
Wool of bat, and tongue of dog,
Adder's fork, and blind-worm's sting,
Lizard's leg, and owlet's wing,
For a charm of powerful trouble,
Like a hell-broth boil and bubble.

Double, double toil and trouble;
Fire burn, and caldron bubble.

William Shakespeare

How to Teach Poetry Writing: Workshops for Ages 8–13, 2nd edn, Routledge © Michaela Morgan 2011

Dinner on Elm Street

Thrice the old school cat hath spewed.
Teachers shriek and children whine:
Ring the bell! 'Tis time! 'Tis time!

Round about the cauldron go,
In the mouldy cabbage throw,
Stone-cold custard, thick with lumps,
Germs from Kevin (sick with mumps).
Boil up sprouts for the greenish smell,
add sweaty sock, cheese pie as well.

Froth and splutter, boil and bubble.
March them in here at the double.

Fillet of an ancient steak
In the cauldron boil and bake.
Eye of spud and spawn of frog,
A chocolate moose, a heated dog.
Add the goo from 'twixt the toes
And crusty bits from round the nose.

Froth and splutter, boil and bubble.
March them in here at the double.

Lumpy mincemeat, grey and gristly,
Giblets, gizzards, all things grizzly.
Beak of chicken in a nugget,
with greasy chips the kids will love it.
Scab of knee sprinkle in,
squeeze juice of pimple from a chin.
Here's the spell 'twill make you thinner.
It's the nightmare Elm Street dinner.

Froth and splutter, boil and bubble.
March them in here at the double!

Michaela Morgan

How to Teach Poetry Writing: Workshops for Ages 8–13, 2nd edn, Routledge © Michaela Morgan 2011

Workshop 16: Hubble Bubble

Read! speak! listen! enjoy!

- Display the poem so that the whole class can see it. If you use a visualiser or an interactive whiteboard, keep a printed copy on display so that children can look at the poem repeatedly and in their own time.
- Group reads refrain.
- Enjoy!

Discuss

- Who wrote these poems?
- How old do you think the poems are? What clues can you find to their age? (name of poet, subject matter, style, words used, form). Pupils can research Shakespeare's dates and background.

Analyse model

- Read the poem modelled on Shakespeare. What similarities can you find? (similar words, rhythm, rhyme scheme, use of refrain, mood).
- Both poems have a strong rhyme and rhythm. Find the rhymes and beat out the rhythm. Both have refrains. Find and compare these.

Write

- **Whole-class activity: write a spell using a writing frame.**
  - Make up refrains. For example:

    > Stir and chop, stir and chop
    > Add it to the cooking pot.
    > Boil and steam, boil and steam
    > Here's a spell to make you scream.

    – Teacher as scribe.

    – Attempt to complete the writing frame at the end of the workshop.

    – List possible ingredients and encourage the addition of adjectives.

    – Spot opportunities for rhyme and alliteration.

    – Encourage the use of a thesaurus or cookery book (to find suitable culinary terms, e.g. *stir in, blend, chop, heat, eat, slice, grate, grind, bake, bind, mix, make, sprinkle, bake, roast, toast, fry,* etc.).

    – Encourage the use of a rhyming dictionary.

- **Move on to independent work.**

    – Pupils to write spells with or without the writing frame. Even when using the frame, some modifications to the frame should be allowed. The frame is a support not a straitjacket! It should provide a starting point.

    – Possible subjects for spells:

        'A Spell to Make a Perfect Poem' (ingredients: rhythm, rhyme etc.)

        'A Spell to Make an Adventure/Mystery/Science-Fiction Story' (following discussion of genres of fiction)

        'A Spell to Pollute the Planet'

        'A Spell to Save the Planet'

        'A Spell to Make a Perfect Friend'

Perform! discuss! enjoy! applaud!

Plenary and revision/redrafting

- Read out and comment on particularly good choices of words.
- Make the point that poems are worked and reworked. Can anyone suggest improvements or alternatives?
- Points to consider: maintaining a rhythm; deleting or adding words; using strong adjectives; re-ordering words and lines for better effect; using a variety of synonyms – culinary terms – as well as *add*; using punctuation.
- Incorporate revisions.
- Ask children to write out or key in their poems – with revisions incorporated.
- Present as a collection or as a display. You could also record or film the performance (see p. 3).

Possibilities for follow-up and cross-curricular links

Instead of writing a spell, write a recipe. This is less challenging as it does not require a grasp of the rhyme and rhythm scheme (see Appendix: 'Recipe for a Story', an example of a Recipe Poem).

    Link spells with other areas of the curriculum (e.g. A Spell to Pollute the Planet. A Spell to make a Viking Warrior).

Spell

Round about the _____ go:

In the _____ throw.

_____

_____

_____

Boil thou first in the charmed pot.

(Refrain): _____

_____

_____

In the cauldron boil and _____

_____

_____

_____

For a charm of powerful trouble,

Like a hell broth boil and bubble.

(Refrain): _____

_____

The Charge of the Light Brigade

Half a league, half a league,
Half a league onward,
All in the valley of Death
Rode the six hundred.
'Forward the Light Brigade!
Charge for the guns!' he said:
Into the valley of Death
Rode the six hundred.
'Forward, the Light Brigade!'
Was there a man dismayed?
Not though the soldier knew
Some one had blundered:
Theirs not to make reply,
Theirs not to reason why,
Theirs but to do and die:
Into the valley of Death
Rode the six hundred.
Cannon to right of them,
Cannon to left of them
Cannon in front of them
Volleyed and thundered;
Stormed at with shot and shell,
Boldly they rode and well,
Into the jaws of Death,
Into the mouth of Hell
Rode the six hundred.

Flashed all their sabres bare,
Flashed as they turned in air
Sabring the gunners there,
Charging an army, while
All the world wondered:
Plunged in the battery-smoke
Right through the line they broke;
Cossack and Russian
Reeled from the sabre-stroke
Shattered and sundered.
Then they rode back, but not
Not the six hundred.
Cannon to right of them,
Cannon to left of them,
Cannon behind them
Volleyed and thundered;
Stormed at with shot and shell,
While horse and hero fell,
They that had fought so well
Came through the jaws of Death,
Back from the mouth of Hell,
All that was left of them,
Left of six hundred.
When can their glory fade?
O the wild charge they made!
All the world wondered.
Honour the charge they made!
Honour the Light Brigade,
Noble six hundred!

Alfred, Lord Tennyson

How to Teach Poetry Writing: Workshops for Ages 8–13, 2nd edn, Routledge © Michaela Morgan 2011

Workshop 17: The Charge of the Light Brigade

Read! speak! listen! enjoy!

- Display the poem so that the whole class can see it. If you use a visualiser or an interactive whiteboard, keep a printed copy on display so that children can look at the poem repeatedly and in their own time.
- Read the verse aloud. Different pupils read, either individually or in groups. This is an easy to understand, action-packed narrative poem, which is not often presented to contemporary children, but many will enjoy its energy and conviction.
- Enjoy!

Discuss

- This is a narrative poem that was once the most popular poem in Britain and then fell out of fashion. It is by a former poet laureate Lord, Alfred Tennyson (1809–1892). Discuss the role of the laureate and compare to the current holder of the post (see p. 65 to read 'Three', a poem by the current poet laureate.)
- Briefly fill in the historic background. The poem deals with an infamous true incident in the Crimean War. Misinterpreted or mistaken orders were obeyed. This led to the Light Brigade making a charge down a heavily defended valley. The men had to ride through cannon fire. Few survived.
- On reading about this incident in a newspaper, Tennyson quickly wrote this poem – it immediately became tremendously popular. It was printed out and passed hand to hand until soldiers still based in the Crimean Peninsular were reading the poem to each other.
- Together with the class, discuss and retell the story of the poem.
  Some vocabulary that may need explaining:

  - league (a measure of distance)
  - Light Brigade (cavalry bearing light arms such as swords)
  - blundered (made a mistake)
  - sabre (type of sword; see also 'sabring')

- Discuss the form of the poem, its rhymes and near-rhymes (onward/hundred), its repetitions, its galloping rhythm and its strong verbs.
- Look at the first two lines (half a league, half a league, half a league onward). Why has the poet chosen to repeat himself (it alters the pace and sounds like hoof beats relentlessly advancing). Find other repeats and discuss how effective a repeat used *intentionally* can be.

Analyse model

Consider and discuss the choice of words. Make a list of strong verbs (volleyed, thundered, stormed, shattered, flashed, plunged etc). These are such strong verbs that they do not need adverbs. It would be repetitive to write 'thundered loudly' or 'flashed quickly'. These additional adjectives would slow down the galloping pace. A good poet edits out *unnecessary* repetition but keeps repetition that adds to the effect.

Write

- **Whole-class activity: writing frame**
  - As a warm up, start with the writing frame (on p. 86) and find two lines that can complete this frame, fit with the rhyme scheme and, importantly, *maintain the mood*.

It is easy, when rhyming, to fall into the trap of losing the mood and falling into unintentional humour. Try various possibilities of rhyming lines and see the effects they have. Demonstrate how there is always more than one choice that can be made, and if you are using rhyme careful choice is very important.

Make a list of words and ideas you might consider using. (Some words/ideas: sight, night, shell, tell, well, fell.)

Example: *Flashing their sabres bright/Riding with all their might.*

Example that shows the pitfalls of rhyme – how rhyme can easily have a comic effect: *Oh what a tale to tell/Didn't they all do well!*

Possibilities for follow-up and cross-curricular links

- **Write a poem based on a true or historic incident.**
  - Imagine you are Poet Laureate and want to write a poem to celebrate an event. This could be a mythical event or an historic event.
  - Research an event that links in with your areas of study.
  - Make notes of key incidents. Make a list of strong words and lines and attempt to tell the story in a narrative poem. Your poem could celebrate a famous football victory, an invention, a discovery, an expedition. You could give your poem a strong refrain – as Tennyson has done with 'The Charge of the Light Brigade'.
  - Below is an idea that will link to a study of the Second World War.

The Dunkirk evacuation
Notes:
The facts:
26 May 1940 to 4 June 1940. Epic rescue.

Beaches in the north of France. Soldiers (from Britain, Canada and Belgium) trapped on the beaches of Dunkirk in northern France. Enemy troops were advancing on them and they were being dive-bombed from the sky.

They could not advance and they could not escape. Behind them lay the sea. The waters near the beach of Dunkirk were too shallow to permit naval rescue boats.

In Operation Dynamo, 'little ships' were called in to help. Any boat bigger than 30 feet was called on to help. A flotilla of small boats, such as ferries, fishing boats and pleasure boats, set off from Britain, and amid fire, over mines and through danger they went backward and forward ferrying the soldiers to safety. Over 330,000 soldiers were saved in this way.

This is where the phrase 'Dunkirk spirit' comes from. It is also sometimes called the 'miracle' of Dunkirk.

Ideas and words to help enrich your poem

Look at a map of Britain and make a list of the towns the boats may have set off from. Specific detail and names can help to make a poem more effective. You can include the names of seaside towns in the rescue poem (e.g. *from Brighton and from Eastbourne, from Hastings and from Battle, from Beachy Head and Leigh on Sea, the little boats set out to sea . . .*).

You might also like to imagine the people involved in this rescue and give them names (e.g. *Uncle Ted, Mr Jones, the postman and his son. Harry and Tony, Arthur and Frank*). You can use these names in the poem.

Look up types of boats and make a list of the sorts of boats that could have been involved, e.g. fishing boats, pleasure boats, tiny boats, ferry boats, cockle boats, racing yachts, merchant ships, sloops, tugs, lifeboats. You can also look up the names of some of the boats that took part (*Renown, Reliant, Resolute, Defender* were some of the names but there were also more 'holiday boat' names like the *Skylark, Bluebird, Lazy Days* and *Pudge*). You can use these names in the poem.

Think of the people sailing these little boats – they were not professional army or navy men. You could imagine what they did in life – maybe they were teachers or dentists or fishermen, tailors, dads and grandads. They navigated their way by following the stench of the smoke, the sound of explosions and the fires on the horizon. They were dive-bombed from above and they were sailing over mines.

The men they found on the beaches of Dunkirk were exhausted and desperate. Many were standing in the water waiting for help.

Useful words, ideas and phrases

- Collective nouns for the group of ships – armada, flotilla, fleet, rag tag, rag bag, hotch-potch, allsorts, pick 'n' mix of ships.
- Other words: sitting ducks, sitting targets, shuttle, to and fro, on the edge, the brink.

- You could make up a refrain based on the refrain in 'The Charge of the Light Brigade' (e.g. *Before them, the enemy/Behind them the grey cold sea/Forward they could not go* or *Planes overhead. Submarines below*).

Follow-up reading and websites

- *The Snow Goose* by Paul Gallico (fiction).
- *The Little Ships* by Louise Borden and Michael Foreman (fiction).
- *My Uncle's Dunkirk* by Mick Manning and Brita Granstrom (non-fiction) (www.timesonline.co.uk/tol/life_and_style/court_and_social/article7113143.ece).
- http://www.encyclopedia.com/topic/Dunkirk.aspx

Perform! discuss! enjoy! applaud!

- Read out the lines, verses or poems composed and comment on particularly good choices of words.
- Make the point that poems are worked and reworked. Can anyone suggest improvements or alternatives?
- Incorporate revisions.
- Ask children to write or type out their lines – with revisions incorporated.
- Present as a collection or display. Consider inviting parents, grandparents and great-grandparents to see displays or performances.

Cannon to right of them,

Cannon to left of them

Cannon in front of them

Volleyed and thundered;

_____

_____

Into the jaws of Death,

Into the mouth of Hell

Rode the six hundred.

The Dead Quire

I

Beside the Mead of Memories,
Where Church-way mounts to
  Moaning Hill,
The sad man sighed his
  phantasies –
He seems to sigh them still.

II

"'Twas the Birth-tide Eve, and the
  hamleteers
Made merry with ancient
  Mellstock zest,
But the Mellstock quire of former
  years
Had entered into rest.

III

"Old Dewy lay by the gaunt yew
  tree,
And Reuben and Michael a pace
  behind,
And Bowman with his family
By the wall that the ivies bind.

IV

"The singers had followed one by
  one,
Treble, and tenor, and thorough-
  bass;
And the worm that wasteth had
  begun
To mine their mouldering place.

V

"For two-score years, ere Christ-
  day light,
Mellstock had throbbed to strains
  from these:
But now there echoed on the
  night
No Christmas harmonies.

VI

"Three meadows off, at a
  dormered inn,
The youth had gathered in high
  carouse,
And, ranged on settles, some
  therein
Had drunk them to a drowse.

VII

"Loud, lively, reckless, some had
  grown,
Each dandling on his jigging knee
Eliza, Dolly, Nance, or Joan –
Livers in levity.

VIII

"The taper flames and hearthfire
  shine
Grew smoke-hazed to a lurid
  light,
And songs on subjects not divine
Were warbled forth that night.

How to Teach Poetry Writing: Workshops for Ages 8–13, 2nd edn, Routledge © Michaela Morgan 2011

IX

"Yet many were sons and
    grandsons here
Of those who, on such eves gone
    by,
At that still hour had throated
    clear
Their anthems to the sky.

X

"The clock belled midnight; and
    ere long
One shouted,'Now 'tis Christmas
    morn;
Here's to our women old and
    young,
And to John Barleycorn!'

XI

"They drink the toast and shout
    again;
The pewter-ware rings back the
    boom,
And for a breath-while follows
    then
A silence in the room.

XII

"When nigh without, as in old
    days,
The ancient quire of voice and
    string
Seemed singing words of prayer
    and praise
As they had used to sing:

XIII

"While shepherds watch'd
    their flocks by night, –
Thus swells the long familiar
    sound
In many a quaint symphonic
    flight –
To, Glory shone around.

XIV

"The sons defined their fathers'
    tones,
The widow his whom she had
    wed,
And others in the minor moans
The viols of the dead.

XV

"Something supernal has the
    sound
As verse by verse the strain
    proceeds,
And stilly staring on the ground
Each roysterer holds and heeds.

XVI

"Towards its chorded closing bar
Plaintively, thinly, waned the
    hymn,
Yet lingered, like the notes afar
Of banded seraphim.

XVII

"With brows abashed, and
    reverent tread,
The hearkeners sought the tavern
    door:
But nothing, save wan moonlight,
    spread
The empty highway o'er.

How to Teach Poetry Writing: Workshops for Ages 8–13, 2nd edn, Routledge © Michaela Morgan 2011

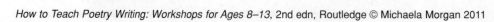

XVIII

"While on their bearing fixed and
    tense
The aerial music seemed to sink,
As it were gently moving thence
Along the river brink.

XIX

"Then did the Quick pursue the
    Dead
By crystal Froom that crinkles
    there;
And still the viewless quire ahead
Voiced the old holy air.

XX

"By Bank-walk wicket, brightly
    bleached,
It passed, and 'twixt the hedges
    twain,
Dogged by the living; till it
    reached
The bottom of Church Lane.

XXI

"There at the turning, it was heard
Drawing to where the churchyard
    lay:
But when they followed
    thitherward
It smalled, and died away.

XXII

"Each gravestone of the quire,
    each mound,
Confronted them beneath the
    moon;
But no more floated therearound
That ancient Birth-night tune.

XXIII

"There Dewy lay by the gaunt
    yew tree,
There Reuben and Michael, a pace
    behind,
And Bowman with his family
By the wall that the ivies bind . . .

XXIV

"As from a dream each sobered
    son
Awoke, and musing reached his
    door;
'Twas said that of them all, not
    one
Sat in a tavern more."

XXV

– The sad man ceased; and ceased
    to heed
His listener, and crossed the leaze
From Moaning Hill towards the
    mead –
The Mead of Memories.

Thomas Hardy

How to Teach Poetry Writing: Workshops for Ages 8–13, 2nd edn, Routledge © Michaela Morgan 2011

Workshop 18: The Dead Quire

Challenging narrative poetry
Ballad
Language change over time
In-depth discussion and analysis of a challenging poem

Read! speak! listen! enjoy!

- Display the poem so that the whole class can see it. If you use a visualiser or an interactive whiteboard, keep a printed copy on display so that children can look at the poem repeatedly and in their own time.
- Read the poem aloud with appropriate expression.
- This is a longer narrative poem – a classic. Explain to the children that there may be many unfamiliar words and it may not be completely clear on first reading – but they can just listen and enjoy the sound, the mood and the general impression.
- Enjoy!

Discuss

- Who wrote this poem?
- How old do you think the poem is? (Thomas Hardy lived from 1840 to 1928 but this poem seems even older. The poet has given it an antique feel by using a traditional form and subject matter, and archaic vocabulary (*'Twas, ere, nigh*, etc.).)
- What clues can you find to the age of this poem? (subject matter, form, style, words used, spellings. Point out that meanings of words and spellings of words have changed over time. Look for examples of these in the poem and demonstrate the contemporary spelling).
- The length of the poem – poems can be very short or very long. This is a narrative poem, which means that it tells a story. This type of poem is often long.
- Rhyme. A poem has carefully chosen words – sometimes the words are chosen to rhyme, sometimes they are chosen for their meaning, sometimes for their sound/music or alliteration. Discuss the rhyme scheme in this poem (it goes *abab*).
- Each stanza is a quatrain, having four lines. This is the traditional form of the ballad – an antique storytelling poem.

Analyse model

Explain that this is a challenging poem and was not written specifically for children.

Select and focus on *some* of these aspects – *too extensive and intensive a study risks deadening the poem*. You can return to the poem from time to time to make further points.

Set the children the tasks of being detectives (C.I.A. Mellstock!) and give groups of children some clues to follow – i.e. some of the following questions to find answers to.

Divide questions so that different ability groups have tasks and quantities of questions appropriate to their capabilities.

- What is the plot of this poem? Attempt to extract and retell the story. Set the children the task of being detectives investigating the incident. The clues will be easier to follow if they consider the following ten questions. Children can work in pairs investigating a specific question and finding lines to produce as evidence to prove their conclusions.
  - Who is telling this tale? (see stanzas I and XXV).
  - What time of year is it?
  - What does 'entered into rest' mean (see stanza II).
  - Where is the choir? (see stanzas III and IV).
  - What are the names of the members of the choir? (see stanza III).
  - How long have they been dead? (see stanza V).
  - What are the young villagers doing? (see stanzas VI, VII and VIII).
  - What happens in stanzas XII to XVI?
  - In XIX the live revellers run after the ghostly choir. What is the name of the river they run beside?
  - XXIII is a repeated stanza (see stanza III). Discuss repetition – why do you think the poet repeats himself? Is this a mistake or intentional?
  - Discuss the final stanza. Is it an effective ending? Does it repeat a previous stanza? Discuss the importance of endings and beginnings. Point out the circularity of some tales – how ending where you began can be a satisfying conclusion to a story or a poem.
- Vocabulary.
  - Some of the vocabulary in this poem will be strange to contemporary children. You have travelled back in time with this poem and you have to guess at some of the word meanings. Guess the meaning of some of the vocabulary, e.g. *Birth-tide Eve, Christ-day light, hearthfire shrine, throated, clock belled midnight, John Barleycorn, a breath-while, stilly, the Quick...the Dead, smalled.*
  - Physically demonstrate some of the vocabulary, for example ask children to move as described in stanza *XVII with brows abashed and reverent tread.*
  - Ask the children to be dictionary detectives. Give groups of children particular words to look up, then ask them to report back to the class explaining any unfamiliar language. Some of the words to investigate are: *mead, phantasies* (note how the spelling has changed over time), *hamleteers* (look up *hamlet*), *zest, gaunt, two-score* (look up *score*), *carouse, levity, taper, warbled, anthems, viols.*
- Find examples of alliteration.
- Find examples of compound descriptions (as in kennings), for example *a breath-while*.
- Ask children to make notes and then orally retell the tale as a spooky story.

- Pick out a word or phrase you like, e.g. *He seems to sigh them still.* Write it down. In plenary, read out your choice and explain what you like about it, e.g. the sound, choice of word, the mood.
- Can you find a line that sounds noisy? One that sounds quiet? What sounds sound quiet? (usually the letter *s* or other soft sounds). Which letters make a noisy sound?

Write

- **Whole-class activity: add a stanza using a writing frame.**
  - Attempt to add a stanza to the poem by completing the writing frame at the end of the workshop.
  - Subjects to start with might be:
    what the drinkers felt like when they heard the choir
    a fuller description of the drinkers following
    the ghostly choir
    the weather
    how the ghostly choir looked.
  - A rhyming dictionary can be of help. *The Penguin Rhyming Dictionary* is fairly easy to use. Use it to look up *night, pale, pane, dark.* Collect rhyming words and list them. Here are some of the words you might come up with: ***night***, *white, moonlight, fright, sight, tight, plight, fight, might, mite;* ***pale***, *frail, trail, sail, fail, stale, vale, veil, wail;* ***pane***, *pain, lane, insane, train, wane, mane, main;* ***dark***, *bark, park, lark, hark, stark.*
  - Use these words to help you to compose a stanza (or more!).
- **Move on to independent work.**
  - Individual children can rewrite the poem as a spooky story – using some of the vocabulary from the poem. Make notes of the story outline in the preparations.
  - The story can be brought up to date – retold in a contemporary setting.
  - The poem has the song-like structure of a ballad. The story can be retold as a modern song, for example as a rap or as a country-and-western song.
  - Retell a story you know as a ballad.

Perform! discuss! enjoy! applaud!

Plenary and revision/redrafting

- Read out and comment on particularly good choices of words.
- Make the point that poems are worked and reworked. Can anyone suggest improvements or alternatives?
- Incorporate revisions.
- Ask children to write or type out their lines – with revisions incorporated.
- Present as a collection or display. You could also record or film the performance (see p. 3).

Possibilities for follow-up and cross-curricular links

Take the opportunity to teach or revise roman numerals (www.romannumerals.co.uk).
Look at traditional ballads and other narrative poems.

Suggested traditional narrative poems to enjoy together are:

'The Listeners' by Walter de la Mare
'The Highwayman' by Alfred Noyes
'The Pied Piper of Hamelin' by Robert Browning
'The Raven' by Edgar Allan Poe
'Robin Hood' ballads (Anon)

Search out more modern narrative poems (e.g. 'Timothy Winters' by Charles Causley).
Make a collection or performance of them.
Collect and read other poems by Thomas Hardy.

The Dead Quire

You can approach this activity by doing the two rhyming lines first.

_____ (a)

_____ (b)

_____ (a)

_____ (b)

_____ (a)

The trees were black in the sky _____ (b)

_____ (a)

The wind was a distant sigh. _____ (b)

Here are some other lines to start you off.

> The ground was white and hard with cold
> The churchyard mossy, dank and old.

> The choristers were ghastly pale
> The air around them earthy stale.

How to Teach Poetry Writing: Workshops for Ages 8–13, 2nd edn, Routledge © Michaela Morgan 2011

Appendix

Figuratively Speaking

"Time to pull out all the stops,"
said the football coach.

"What do you mean?" I asked.

"Put your shoulder to the wheel," he explained,

"and your nose to the grindstone."

"What wheel? What grindstone?" I wondered.

"Keep your eye on the ball."

"I can do that," I said. "No problem."

"Chin up," he insisted. "Stiff upper lip."

I answered, "Mmmmmmmmm." But it

was difficult to speak.

"Just hold your tongue, pull your socks up, hop to it and

put your best foot forward."

The coach blew his whistle.

"Argh!" I screamed,

as I tumbled in the mud.

The coach glared at me –

"Can't you follow a simple instruction?"

Michaela Morgan

How to Teach Poetry Writing: Workshops for Ages 8–13, 2nd edn, Routledge © Michaela Morgan 2011

Recipe for a Story

Take an introduction.

Blend in atmosphere.

Stir in description and conversation.

Spice it up with suspense, humour, or adventure.

Allow to rise.

Cook thoroughly, checking it from time to time.

Add the finishing touches – a good final sentence.

Sprinkle with punctuation.

Serve piping hot.

Michaela Morgan

How to Teach Poetry Writing: Workshops for Ages 8–13, 2nd edn, Routledge © Michaela Morgan 2011

Bibliography

Oral and traditional verse

Iona Opie, *People in the Playground,* Oxford University Press.
Iona and Peter Opie, *Children's Games in Street and Playground,* Oxford University Press.
Iona and Peter Opie, *The Lore and Language of Schoolchildren,* Oxford University Press.
Iona and Peter Opie, *The Singing Game,* Oxford University Press.
Brian Wildsmith (illustrated) *Favourite Nursery Rhymes,* Oxford University Press.

Particularly multicultural poems

John Agard and Grace Nichols, *From Mouth to Mouth,* Walker Books. Poems passed from mouth to mouth, from all over the world: Russia, India, Jamaica, Vietnam... There are schoolyard chants, sea shanties, work songs, riddles, spells and curses, and more.
Asian Nursery Rhymes (with CD), Mantra Lingua.
Valerie Bloom, *Ackee, Breadfruit, Callaloo* (a celebration of Caribbean food, life and culture in a verse alphabet), Bogle-l'Ouverture Press.

Nonsense, nursery and early rhymes

Edward Lear, *Book of Nonsense* (this includes limericks and exists in various editions).
Max Fatchen, *Wry Rhymes for Troublesome Times,* Viking Kestrel.
Richard Edwards, *Nonsense Nursery Rhymes,* Oxford University Press.
Richard Edwards, *Nonsense ABC Rhymes,* Oxford University Press.
Richard Edwards, *Nonsense Christmas Rhymes,* Oxford University Press.
Kaye Umansky and Richard Edwards, *Nonsense Fairy Tale Rhymes,* Oxford University Press.
Kaye Umansky and Richard Edwards, *Nonsense Rhymes Collection,* Oxford University Press.
Spike Milligan, *Silly Verse for Kids,* Puffin.
John Foster, *Whizz Bang Orang-Utan,* Oxford University Press.
John Foster, *Twinkle Twinkle Chocolate Bar,* Oxford University Press.
John Foster, *See You Later, Escalator,* Oxford University Press.

Poems to perform

Michaela Morgan (ed.), *Words to Whisper, Words to SHOUT,* Belitha Press.
John Foster (ed.), *Ready Steady Rap,* Oxford University Press.
Clive Sansom (ed.), *Speech Rhymes,* A & C Black.
Paul Cookson (ed.), *Unzip Your Lips,* Macmillan.

Paul Cookson and David Harmer, *Spill the Beans*: *Action-packed Performance Poems*, Macmillan.
Paul Cookson and Nick Toczek, *Read Me Out Loud*, Macmillan.

General collections

Pie Corbett (ed.), *The Works Key Stage 1: Every kind of poem you will ever need for the Literacy Hour*, Macmillan.
Paul Cookson (ed.), *The Works,* Macmillan.
Pie Corbett (ed.), *Poems for Year 3*, Macmillan.
Gaby Morgan (ed.), *Read Me, A Poem a Day*, Macmillan.

Poems linked by theme

Allan Ahlberg, *Friendly Matches Poems* (about football), Viking Kestrel.
David Orme, *'Ere We Go* (football poems), Macmillan.
Collections by John Foster. Themes include: Sports, Ghosts, Space, Night, Snow, Sea, Shape, Food, and many more, Oxford University Press.
John Foster (ed.), *Monster Poems* illustrated by Korky Paul, Oxford University Press.
John Foster (ed.), *Magic Poems* illustrated by Korky Paul, Oxford University Press.
John Foster (ed.), *Pet Poems* illustrated by Korky Paul, Oxford University Press. Also in the same series: *Dragon Poems, Dinosaur Poems, Fantastic Football Poems*, all Oxford University Press.
Clare Bevan has written collections of poems about ballerinas, mermaids, fairies etc., all published by Macmillan.
Fiona Waters, *Red Lorry, Yellow Lorry – poems about cars and trucks and other things that go*, Macmillan.
Gaby Morgan, *Space Poems*, Macmillan.

Riddles, puns, jokes and tongue-twisters

Pie Corbett (ed.), *Footprints in the Butter and other Mysteries, Riddles and Puzzles*, Belitha Press.
Brough Girling (ed.), *The Great Puffin Joke Dictionary*, Puffin.
Paul Cookson (ed.), *Tongue Twisters and Tonsil Twizzlers*, Macmillan.
Paul Cookson (ed.), *Let's Twist Again: More Tongue Twisters and Tonsil Twizzlers*, Macmillan.

Some useful websites

http://www.poetryarchive.org/poetryarchive/teachersHome.do
http://poetryzone.co.uk/
www.poetrysociety.org.uk
http://performapoem.lgfl.org.uk
http://www.thepoetrychannel.org.uk